Endorsements

Henry not only speaks to men showing them there is hope — help for a way out of the bondage of pornography, but he does it from a compassionate and understanding heart. He understands the battles — he knows how to win the war. Victory is assured for the man who knows God.

However, this is not a book just for men. Women need to understand the war that men wage every day. The insights in this book can enable them to be more understanding to help their sons, husbands, and brothers to know how to pray. Women also need to understand that men are turned on by sight. They are not "dirty-minded men" — they are men! And we have a duty as women to dress what befits a woman of God rather than the culture.

> Kay Arthur
> Precept Ministries

The Silent War is a book for such a time as this. As a 25-year former pornography addict, I wish that I had read a book like this before the addiction took root.

> Phil Burress, President
> Citizens for Community Values

The Silent War addresses a very sensitive and critical subject with both biblical accuracy and compassion. It does not take lightly the severity of sin and at the same time explains and applauds God's complete ability to give victory over temptation and addiction. On the subject of sexual temptation, it's a must-read.

> R. Larry Moyer, President and CEO
> EvanTell, Inc.

Sad to say, many families, including Christian, are being torn apart by the use of pornography. Henry Rogers understands this battle from personal experience and shares with compassion how to be free from its stranglehold.

> Beverly LaHaye, Founder and Chairman
> Concerned Women for America

The
Silent War

Ministering to Those Trapped
in the Deception of Pornography

HENRY J. ROGERS

New Leaf Press

First printing: January 2000
Second printing: June 2001

ISBN: 0-89221-491-0
Library of Congress Catalog Card Number: 99-69241

Printed in the United States of America.

Our appreciation to Thomas Nelson Publishers, Nashville, Tennessee, for permission to reprint the prayer by Charles Stanely which begins on page 206.

Please visit our website for other great titles:
www.newleafpress.net

For information regarding publicity for author interviews contact Dianna Fletcher at (870) 438-5288.

Dedication

In loving memory of my brother,
Robert Alexander Rogers.

*Let your father and your mother be
glad, and let her rejoice who gave birth
to you* (Prov. 23:25).

Acknowledgments

This is the fun part of writing . . . thanking the people who helped make this possible! I used to think that God put Kerby Anderson in my path to help me get this book published. I couldn't have done it without him and was amazed that he was willing to invest time in a would-be author that he hardly knew. After all, he is an author, nationally syndicated talk show host, and president of Probe Ministries. And me? I'm not even a household name on my street. That didn't seem to matter to Kerby, though.

I'll never forget the day he asked me for book proposals to pass out to various publishers. Over time Kerby became much more than the cheapest literary agent ever to get a book published. He became my friend.

Every book needs an editor. Violet Vickery spent hours going over my manuscript armed only with a red pen. It's a weapon she knows how to use well. If editing were an Olympic event, she would bring home the gold. She is more than an editor, though. She, too, is a dear friend and prayer warrior who took on the project because of our friendship.

Working for Norm Miller, the chairman of the board for Interstate Batteries, is a joy. His trust and confidence in me is humbling. I remember when we went together to a Texas prison to participate in a Bill Glass Weekend of Champions. We were teamed together in maximum security as we shared our faith with inmates. When I finished talking to one inmate I saw Norm, several cells away, on his knees on the concrete floor, talking to another inmate. That picture has been photographed on the table of my heart. He inspires me to grow in my relationship with Christ by the way he lives.

Dan Panetti and Julie Lunsford from the Dallas Association for Decency are a wonderful encouragement to me along with the DAD board of directors. I love them all and they are a great team that is making a difference in Dallas . . . for the sake of our families.

In Memphis, Carolyn McKenzie from Citizens for Community Values was a huge help in allowing me the opportunity to talk with women who were once part of but now out of the sex industry. Her heart for these women is bigger than the state of Texas.

Of course, I would be remiss if I forgot two champions of the decency fight. El Arnold is the founder of the Dallas Association for Decency, and retired FBI agent Bill Kelly has been involved in the fight for years. El Arnold inspired my passion for making a difference and Bill Kelly has been a tireless source of support.

Landra Carroll is my assistant at Interstate Batteries. Not only is she a trusted co-worker, but she accompanied me on several interviews with women from the adult entertainment industry. She models for me the heart of a servant.

I'm thankful to Jim and Dianna Fletcher, Judy Lewis, and Janell Robertson at New Leaf Press who took a risk on a new author writing about a difficult and sensitive subject. I appreciate the excellent work they do.

I am blessed to serve as an associate pastor at Lawson Road Baptist Church. My wonderful church family is such an encouragement to me. They are a loving group of people and a joy to worship with. My pastor, Richard Harris, is not only my co-laborer in Christ, he is my friend.

The one who had the greatest confidence in me is my loving wife, Kathy. Writing a book is time-consuming and requires great sacrifice. In the four years of research and writing, Kathy never complained. All she knows how to do is encourage. She is indeed my reward in life (Eccles. 9:9).

I want to thank my children Gabrielle, Whitney, and Henry Jr. who make fatherhood a blessing. One of my greatest joys in life is hearing them say the word "Daddy."

Finally, I want to thank God for His faithfulness and for providing men with a way of escape (1 Cor. 10:13). My prayer is that God would be glorified and men would be changed.

Contents

Forewords by Norm Miller 11

and Kerby Anderson

Introduction: A License to Lust 15

1. Regarding Henry 23

2. A Defining Moment 31

3. We're at War 43

4. She Has a Name 67

5. Where in the World Is Ward Cleaver? 89

6. Satan's Dynamic Duo: Hugh and Larry 97

7. VCR — Very Corrupt Rendevouz 109

8. Sorry, Wrong Number 119

9. The Internet — The Brave New World of Porn ... 129

10. A Place for "Gentlemen" 149

11. Her Name Is Not Barbie 161

12. The Lust of the Flesh — A Day of Vice 169

13. The Peril of Pornography 177

14. Triumph over Temptation 193

15. "But This Is My Daddy" 221

16. The Wounded Wife 231

Epilogue: Loose Ends 235

Forewords

IT WAS ALMOST TWO YEARS AGO when we needed to replace our corporate chaplain at Interstate Batteries. With our home office being in Dallas, many expected us to turn to one of the local seminaries. But I had known Henry for the past eight years, since he came on board with Interstate's Human Resources Department. I had noticed his pastor's heart and was impressed with the way he ministered to our employees through relationships and Bible studies. Here's a man who never received a seminary education but has proved faithful in handling the Word of God and equipping the saints.

Henry has a habit of leading a person back to the Scriptures. And he's not afraid to ask the tough questions, which explains his courage to address an issue that so many men deal with but so few want to discuss. Even in writing this book, he's going against the flow and touching something that many men would just as soon leave untouched. Sexual temptation has an ever-increasing impact in the lives of Christian men and Henry gets to the root of the problem with confidentiality, compassion, and love.

His passion is for the spiritual wholeness of the family, and that's why he's so active in his fight against pornography and sexual lust. He's told me how he has seen it destroy families by crushing the self-esteem of the wife, enslaving the husband, and diminishing the marriage relationship. He is also very much concerned for those who are involved in this destructive industry, and has the desire and the wisdom to help men find victory over pornography.

Henry is serious about this issue, but he has a way of looking to the positive in almost any situation, which is why I enjoy being around him. Best of all, he's devoted to his wife and kids.

He is one of the most genuine people I know, sincerely warm and compassionate, a true friend. He's willing to confront, spiritually challenge, and spur folks on in their spiritual growth. He knows that God's desire is for all of us to be victorious in times of temptation. Read his book. It will help you and many other men find victory.

Norm Miller
Chairman of the Board
Interstate Battery Corp.

SEXUAL TEMPTATION HAS ALWAYS been with us. After all, lust is listed as one of the seven deadly sins. But in recent decades the odds have been stacked against us in this war of sexual tempation.

Today, adult bookstores outnumber McDonalds. Video stores rent and sell titles that wouldn't have even been permitted in their stores a few years ago. Businessmen who would never go to a strip joint are invited to discuss business deals at upscale gentlemen's clubs. And the Internet-linked homes provide the most tantalizing pornography with just a few mouse clicks.

This is the new world of pornography, and Henry Rogers takes us into it. It is a world most of us would like to avoid and ignore. But the fact that you picked up this book is testimony to the fact that you or someone you know enters into this world.

Henry takes us into a world where men peruse video titles in stores often quieter than libraries. He tells the stories of strippers and prostitutes whose lives have been devastated by pornography. And he takes us into the solitary world of on-line pornography and the pseudo-cyber world of chat rooms where men and women reveal their sexual fantasies to each other. It's not a pleasant world, but Henry Rogers exposes it and discusses it with candor, tact, and compassion.

But Henry is not only a tour guide; he is a fellow traveler. Readers will appreciate his vulnerability as he shares how he got caught up in the snare of sexual temptation and found a way of escape (1 Cor. 10:13). There can be victory over sexual temptation, as this book clearly documents.

Buy this book. Read this book. Apply it to your life. We are commanded to flee youthful lusts (2 Tim. 2:22). This book will help you and the people in your life know how to do so. Believe me, the sad stories will give you ample motivation. Get *The Silent War* today so that you aren't another tragic casualty in the war against sexual temptation.

Kerby Anderson
President
Probe Ministries

Introduction

A License to Lust

For by grace you have been saved through faith; and that not of yourselves, it is the gift of God (Eph. 2:8).

WHENEVER I START SOMETHING BIG, I always consult with my wife, Kathy. I have found that her confirmation is important for matters I believe God has put on my heart. If Kathy is not in agreement with me, I reexamine my desire. One night we were sitting on the couch and, out of the blue, I told her I wanted to write a book about pornography and sexual temptation. I had taught a seminar and written a booklet on temptation so I hoped it would sound like a good idea to her.

Kathy's approval was confirmed when she said, "Henry, that sounds good, but do me one favor." I told her I would do anything and she said, "Don't dedicate the book to me." The comment was meant as a joke, but it spoke volumes to me. The very thought of pornography is repulsive to many women. Repulsive to women, yet it can be so addictive to men.

I have spoken to women whose husbands are addicted and others whose marriages were destroyed because of their husband's addiction. Replacing the desire for our wives with the video-enhanced women found in pornography cuts our wives at the core. One woman I spoke to said her husband read pornographic magazines all their married life. Amazingly, she told me that her husband doesn't think it bothers her. In a moment of confidence and transparency, she confessed that she has hated his addiction for years.

In his letter to the church at Ephesus, Paul wrote, "Husbands, love your wives, just as Christ also loved the church and gave himself up for her" (Eph. 5:25). How much did Christ love the church? Enough to die for her. Guys, are we willing to die for our wives? Obviously not. Too many Christian men have replaced the desire for their wives with pornography and adult entertainment. Is it any wonder that marriages are failing and our marriage vows ring hollow?

What about single men? Do bachelors have a green light because they do not have wives? Certainly not. The apostle Paul tells men to "flee youthful lusts" (2 Tim. 2:22). Can single men honestly believe that this addiction ends at the marriage altar? Unfortunately, the addiction does not end at the altar. In many cases, it gets worse. The difference is that married men begin to hurt the ones they love. That's quite a price to pay for lust.

If you're a man, you know about sexual temptation. It's that simple. Once when I went to Kinko's Copies to have some material run off, I saw a beautiful woman in a skimpy halter-top. Her buxom figure made me wonder if she was a stripper. Instead of continuing to stare, I decided to go sit down while waiting for my order to be completed. I sat down with my back to this woman.

A man sat down next to me and instantly said upon seeing this beautiful woman, "Oh my, now I know why I like to come to Dallas. She's a good-looking woman!" The comment was meant for me but I didn't want to respond. What would I say — "Boy she sure is! I just finished battling with lust myself." I decided to pretend I hadn't heard him.

I could see out of the corner of my eye that his gaze was still fixed in her direction.

It amazed me that men feel lust is an open topic for discussion . . . even for strangers. There was no shame in this man lusting and verbalizing his lust to a complete stranger, though he did seem a bit embarrassed later in our conversation when I told him I was a chaplain. Though still not right, this was conversation once reserved for the locker room. Today, however, lust has found its way into our daily conversations.

My desire to write about the subject is simple. I believe pornography and sexual temptation is ripping the soul out of the American male. Many men today have a love/hate relationship with pornography that is destroying families. A Christian counselor in Dallas told me that the number of her clients trapped in pornography addiction has increased significantly in the past ten years. If they loved pornography they wouldn't be seeing her. If they hated pornography they wouldn't be seeing her. The reason these men go to a counselor is because they love *and* hate pornography.

We are bombarded by sexual messages today like never before, through mediums that our great-grandparents could never have imagined. Billy Graham was on target when he said, "To read the papers and magazines you would think we were almost worshiping the female bosom."[1] Our culture has given us a license to lust. Yet within the hearts of Christian men, a battle is raging. God has given those who follow Him no such license.

LIVING ON TOP OF THE BAR

Could you imagine what it would be like to fight an alcohol addiction while living in an apartment on top of a bar? Each day as you walk up the stairs to your apartment you pass slowly by the bar's front door with people inside enjoying themselves. How difficult would that make it for you to be victorious? That is the worst place to live for a man struggling with alcohol!

I believe living in America today is like living on top of the bar for men who struggle with sexual temptation. We are surrounded by sexual images like never before. TV, newspapers, magazines, videos . . . the list goes on.

An editorial for *Adult Video News* reported, "At this point in history, pornography is hip. I know . . . we like to call it 'adult entertainment' because 'porn' has a bad connotation. But guess what? Porn is happening; it's all right to say you like it."[2]

As much as I hate to admit it, the editorial writer is correct. In today's culture, porn is chic. Porn star Nina Hartley, who starred in the acclaimed movie *Boogie Nights*, once lectured at Harvard University. Universities across the country offer "porn studies" in their course load, though they are often hidden under titles like "community studies." Teaching porn is "a good gig if you can get it," said porn star Sharon Mitchell.[3]

Wesleyan University in Connecticut has a course that requires students to produce pornography as their final exam. Hope Weissman, the woman's studies professor of "Pornography: Writing of Prostitutes" declared that "nothing would be considered too risqué" on the final exam.[4] I'm afraid that I would have to disagree with Ms. Weissman when student projects include a re-creation of a sadomasochistic beating and a video showing the eyes of a male student while he masturbates.

Even though Douglas J. Bennet, Wesleyan's president, ordered a review of the course, he said that the course was a good one with a legitimate subject matter.[5] It seems a few people have disconnected their brain at this prestigious Methodist university.

The Center for Sex Research at California State University — Northridge even sponsored the World Pornography Conference in August 1998. The aim of the conference was simple — to celebrate pornography.[6] Sessions included, "Cyberspace and Interactive Sex," "Defending

Sexual Expression," "The Scope of the Adult Phone Service," "A Short History of Sex Toys," "Spanking Stories," and a discussion of Sharon Mitchell's documentary, "Daddy Make Me a Star."

Conference organizers even used porn "actresses" to speak to over 600 attendees, yet none of them talked about the porn stars that were sexually abused as children. One California State instructor led a seminar titled "There Is No Relationship Between Pornography and Violence against Anyone or Anything."

"I think this is very healthy," said conference attendee Gigi Appleton, who runs an adult movie production company. "It validates our industry."[7]

As 1999 began, *The Washington Post* once again published "The List." "The List" appears each New Year's Day. It includes 50 items that are "In" and "Out." Guess what's in for 1999? Yep. *The Washington Post* listed *pornography* and *Hustler Magazine* publisher Larry Flynt as "In" for 1999.[8]

A headline in *USA Today* read, "Denuding New York of Character." The complaint? It seems the insensitive Mayor Rudy Giuliani cleaned up Times Square by removing adult businesses. When the strip clubs and bookstores left, so went the "character" of New York.[9] It appears some people have trouble with the definition of character.

Is porn chic in America? Maybe the most telling proof is the number of obscenity prosecutions. During the Bush presidency there were 223 obscenity prosecutions, but in the first five years of the Clinton presidency, there were only 105 — 32 cases in 1993, 27 in 1994, 21 in 1995, 19 in 1996, and 6 in 1997.[10] Do you see a trend? That's a decline of 86 percent during the Clinton administration. Yes, porn is chic in America.

After the presidential sexual escapades and deception in 1998 and 1999, it may not surprise you that presidential candidate Bill Clinton wrote the following in October 1992 to Betty Wein, senior editor of Morality in Media, Inc.: "Be assured that aggressive enforcement of federal obscenity laws by the Justice Department — particularly by the Child Exploitation and Obscenity Section — will be a priority in a Clinton-Gore administration." A decline of 86 percent is a priority? I'd hate to see what would have happened if the Clinton-Gore administration had not made obscenity enforcement a "priority."

It would be easy to throw up our hands and say fighting the battle is beyond hope. The message and the temptation are overpowering. It is a battle we cannot win. As I drive by a "Gentlemen's Club" near my home, a packed parking lot tells me that many men have lost the battle. Convenience stores with rows of pornography, yet to be sold, tell me that many more will lose the battle in the days to come.

Even men's magazines at the grocery store, with topics on health and fitness, feature articles about sex. I read a new men's magazine that had many articles like you would find in *Gentleman's Quarterly*, but it also had an article called "Referral Sex." Referral sex? What in the world was that? I bought the magazine to learn more. When I finished reading I was dumbfounded.

The female author said that women like to talk about the sex they had with various men. "When it comes to the gal grapevine, news of a man who makes a woman go limp with lust — and satisfaction — travels faster than insider info on Wall Street," wrote Catherine Romano. "And women don't just gab, they act on the info. Here's how to benefit from the buzz."[11] What! This article, written by a woman in a men's magazine, discussed how men can get more women in bed ... as if it was a goal of men today. Is the author way off base or do I have my head in the sand?

Maybe men are just men. We're visual beings and God created this sexual desire in us. Yes, a desire created by God, but perverted by man. In the wake of our perversion we leave a trail of tears from wives with scarred self-esteem and shattered dreams to sons who carry on our addiction into the next generation. And our daughters learn that the way to man's heart is though seduction and sex. All because we surrendered to a lustful addiction rooted in human depravity.

God, however, does not condone our surrender. He has a plan for us to be victorious. The battle will rage until His return, but we need not fill spiritual hospitals with our wounded and dying. Lust is a battle that we will fight and it is battle that we can win. It is a battle we must win.

I'll even go a step farther — its *God's will* that you be victorious. "For this is the will of God, your sanctification; that is, that you abstain from sexual immorality; that each of you know how to possess his own vessel in sanctification and honor, not in lustful passion, like the Gentiles who do not know God" (1 Thess. 4:3–5).

Not only does this verse tell us that it is God's will for us to be victorious, but it also tells us why we shouldn't be surprised that many men have given in to lustful passion. The verse tells us why men engage in sexual immorality by frequenting sexually oriented businesses, buying pornographic videos, calling phone sex lines, and spending time in pornographic web sites on the Internet. They don't know God. That's *their* excuse, but what about *you*?

One question remains. Are you willing to fight? If not, close this book and return it to the bookstore for a refund. However, if you are willing to fight, you have taken a giant step towards victory. We'll simply look at pornography and adult entertainment to see what we're up against. We'll discover a battle plan that can lead to victory. God's plan begins with confession. Take what is now in darkness and bring it into the light.

> And this is the message we have heard from
> Him and announce to you, that God is light, and in
> Him there is no darkness at all. If we say that we
> have fellowship with Him and yet walk in the

darkness, we lie and do not practice the truth; but if we walk in the light as He himself is in the light, we have fellowship with one another, and the blood of Jesus His Son cleanses us from all sin. If we say that we have no sin, we are deceiving ourselves, and the truth is not in us. If we confess our sins, He is faithful and righteous to forgive us our sins and to cleanse us from all unrighteousness. If we say that we have not sinned, we make Him a liar, and His word is not in us (1 John 1:5–10).

Start by asking God to forgive you for the lust of your heart. Ask Him to change you into the man He wants you to be (2 Tim. 2:21). In the days ahead you'll continue to face temptation and you will experience defeat. Your lust wasn't created in a day, and unless God, by His grace, miraculously and instantly frees you of your addiction, you have a tough road ahead. But remember, there is victory at the finish line. See you there.

1 Bruce H. Wilkinson, *Victory over Temptation* (Eugene, OR: Harvest House Publishers, Inc., 1998), p. 229.
2 *Adult Video News*, November 1997.
3 Matt Labash, "Among the Pornographers," *The Weekly Standard*, September 21, 1998.
4 Marlin Maddox, "Pornography as Higher Learning," "Point of View" radio talk show, June 18, 1999.
5 Ibid.
6 Labash, "Among the Pornographers."
7 "Publisher's Daughter Raps Porn as Sex Summit Kicks Off," *Las Vegas Review Journal*, August 9, 1998.
8 "The 1999 List," *Washington Post*, Style Section, p. G1.
9 "Denuding New York of Character," *USA Today*, July 6, 1999, p. 5D.
10 Morality in Media, Inc. release, October 19, 1998.
11 Catherine Romano, "Referral Sex," *Maxim Magazine*, July/August 1998.

1

Regarding Henry

I have made a covenant with my eyes not to
look lustfully at a girl (Job 31:1; NIV).

PEOPLE WHO WRITE BOOKS are normally authorities on their subject. If you read a book about planting flowers, you would expect that the author had plenty of experience and a beautiful yard. If you read a book about politics, you would expect the author to be a seasoned veteran of political campaigns, an author whose insights could lead to victory on the campaign trail.

I hesitate to call myself an authority on pornography and adult entertainment. My exposure would hardly qualify me as an expert. I do know about sexual temptation, however. I also know about defeat. I have felt its sting many times as a teenager and as an adult. Thankfully, I also know about the victory that is found in Jesus Christ.

I grew up with pornography at my fingertips. During my formative junior and senior high years, there were very few issues of *Playboy* and *Penthouse* that escaped my view. Magazines that had been discarded near my home were quickly captured and hidden for another day. In my life, the seeds were planted. They were seeds that took root.

I went to an all-male military college and the bookstore was kind enough to provide my favorite magazines without the fear of being caught by my parents. Now I could buy my own magazines. I could also share with other guys in the barracks. As my fascination with pornography grew, my shame decreased. Upon graduation I was assigned to the Infantry School at Fort Benning, Georgia. The Army post was adjacent to the city of Columbus, which had numerous sexually oriented businesses. Ladies looked just like the ones I had seen in the magazines, except they performed live and in person. I invested countless one-dollar bills in the g-strings of attractive dancers. My weekend calendar became very full.

I remember going to a club by myself once when one of the dancers asked if she could join me. I was a young 21-year-old army officer and a beautiful dancer wanted to sit with me! Wow! As soon as she sat down the waitress suddenly appeared and asked if I wanted something to drink. When I ordered a Coke the waitress asked, "Would you like to order something for the lady?" "Sure," I replied. "What would you like?" She ordered a carafe of wine, which cost me ten bucks. I convinced myself it was worth it because she was so beautiful. I also thought she liked me. In a short time we seemed to hit it off very well.

You would not believe how fast my new friend drank that wine. At these clubs I learned the art of taking an hour to drink a Coke, but my gorgeous dancer knew how to drink a carafe of wine in five minutes. As soon as she took the last sip the waitress appeared again. "Would you like to order the lady something else?" I'm no cheapskate; of course she could have something else. She ordered another carafe of wine. Ten more bucks down the drain. That night I spent 40 dollars for wine that I later found out was colored water. She didn't like me, she liked my wallet. As soon as the money was gone, so was my "new friend." After dumping me, she found another male victim who gladly bought her more "wine."

You might think that after getting ripped off for my stupidity, I would never grace the doors of a sexually oriented business again. No such luck. I had recovered from the embarrassment by the next weekend. The only change was that I was determined to drink my Coke alone.

Watching women dance and strip was exciting, but soon the thrill was gone. I needed something more. I was in another club when a dancer came up behind me and whispered, "Are you ready to party?" "Sure," I replied, as she sat down wearing something that looked like a skimpy cheerleader's outfit. I ordered my usual Coke and she ordered a beer. After a few minutes she asked me if I wanted her to dance for me. I never had a lap dance before so I asked her for the details.

"It's 10 dollars if I dance here at the table," she said. "I won't touch you and you can't touch me." She pointed to a room off to the side that didn't have any doors and said, "If we go in there it is 20 dollars. It's a little more quiet and I'll touch you, but you still can't touch me." I liked the direction this was going as she told me about the third option. "Or we can go upstairs," she said, smiling. "It's very private and we can touch each other." The cost for this option was 30 dollars. My mind was racing as she waited expectantly for an answer. I knew I was negotiating with a stripper but she seemed more like Monty Hall from the television show "Let's Make a Deal." Which door would I choose?

Once again she whispered, "Are you ready to party?" I knew I shouldn't be in the club but a beautiful dancer was whispering in my ear waiting for my answer. That was not the time to make a righteous decision. I had lost the battle to lust before I ever walked into the building. Without looking the dancer in the eyes, I told her I wanted to go upstairs. Once we were on a couch in a secluded room, one dance turned into two and two dances turned into three. After five dances, lasting less than 20 minutes, I handed her $150, almost a third of my monthly take home pay. I was overcome with shame and excitement at the same time.

I thank God because my experience could have been much worse. Several times I was propositioned outside clubs, but for some reason I always declined. This was before herpes and AIDS became well known so I had no real fear of disease. Looking back, I believe God protected me in these experiences.

Maybe your story is worse, but I know what it feels like. After coming to Christ I still was not free from lust but I knew there was hope. There were good days and bad days. Someone once said, "When you flee temptation, don't leave a forwarding address." Unfortunately, I often did more than leave a forwarding address. I packed temptation in my suitcase.

In Romans 7:15, Paul wrote, "For that which I am doing, I do not understand; for I am not practicing what I would like to do, but I am doing the very thing I hate." That verse described me too well. At times I felt trapped. The temptation was overpowering and the only way to make it stop was to give in. Overcome with guilt, temptations left for a short period but always came back with greater force.

What I have discovered is that I am weakest when God is not my top priority. When I am teaching a Sunday school class or listening to a sermon, sexual temptation never even crosses my mind. When I am fervently praying or reading God's word, temptation has no access to my mind. The door slams shut when God fills my thoughts. When I am not reading the Bible or praying regularly, my thoughts will wander much more during the course of the day.

In James 4:8 it is written, "Draw near to God and He will draw near to you. Cleanse your hands, you sinners; and purify your hearts, you double-minded." Doesn't that make sense? If we draw near to God, He draws near to us! As God draws near, temptation is weakened. Of course, I still face temptation today, but in itself temptation is not a sin. The difference is that now I know I can be victorious. I have the power to choose. I no longer "have" to give in. I have also learned that there is great joy in victory over temptation.

I believe my own experience is proof that God's word is true. In 1 Corinthians 10:12–13, Paul wrote, "Therefore let him who thinks he stands take heed lest he fall. No temptation has overtaken you but such as is common to man; and God is faithful, who will not allow you to be tempted beyond what you are able, but with the temptation will provide the way of escape also, so that you will be able to endure it." Those are just two verses but they are packed full of helpful information for the man struggling with sexual temptation. Let's see what Paul tells us.

1. *Don't think for a minute that you cannot fall.* Men who tell me that they do not experience sexual temptation scare me most of all. I know I am just one bad decision from taking a fall. I also know the only thing that can protect me is my obedience to God. My purity is not a matter of pride; it's a matter of prayer and protection.

2. *Temptation's desire is to overtake you.* Temptations are not something out there for you to try to find. Temptation will not only find you, but it can overtake you. I remember playing a football game as a child and I caught a pass and was running as fast as I could for the end zone. Unfortunately, the defender was faster. He overtook me before I scored and grabbed my collar and threw me down hard to the ground. I went down before I got to the end zone. Sexual temptation has overtaken me, too. Like my failed touchdown run, temptation grabbed me and threw me hard to the ground.

3. *Your temptation is common to man.* Every living, breathing man and woman is tempted. You are not

alone. Of course, we are not all tempted by the same thing, but everyone knows about temptation because it is *common to man.* Jesus understands temptation, too, because He was tempted by Satan.

4. *God is faithful.* This is great news! He will not abandon you in the midst of your temptation.

5. *God will only permit what you are able to bear.* How wonderful that God knows how much each of us can take. He will not allow Satan to give you more than you can handle.

6. *God makes a way of escape in every temptation.* I read about a pastor who felt very uncomfortable with a certain woman after church. As he stood in the back of the sanctuary saying goodbye to his congregation, he noticed that this woman always hugged him. He also felt that the hug was much more than a Sunday after-church hug. Knowing God's word, he asked for a way of escape. The next Sunday he saw the woman walking toward him and he asked God once again to show him the way of escape. Suddenly, he felt a pull at his trousers. It was a child. The pastor picked up the child, who filled his arms and didn't allow him to hug this woman. Each Sunday as she headed toward the back of the sanctuary, the pastor looked for the nearest child to hold. God gives us a way of escape . . . look for it.

7. *God will help you bear it.* You will be tempted, but you won't be alone. God will be with you in the midst of the fight.

There is a freeing feeling knowing that we are not alone in our struggle. I facilitate a small group of men who want to be victorious over sexual addiction. When Jeremy spoke at his first meeting and told his story he said he could not believe how good it felt. No one looked at him with shock and amazement. No one questioned his faith. He joyfully discovered that he was not alone. There were other Christian men who knew well the battle he was fighting.

I believe sexual temptation is different than many other temptations. If I struggled with greed, I would not have a problem asking anyone in my church to remember me in prayer as I battled greed. I can say the same thing about gossip, pride, and many other sins. In our minds, however, the sin of sexual lust brings on incredible shame for the Christian man. You would never hear me say at a church elder meeting, "Guys, will you pray for me this week? There is this lady in my neighborhood I have been lusting after." After all, Christian men should not be struggling with lust, right?

Strangely enough, I believe there is also shame for those who don't know Christ. I remember once being in an adult bookstore filled with magazines, videos, and all kinds of gizmos and gadgets. These places are quieter than the local library. Men don't look at each other. If their eyes do meet, they quickly look away. You don't hear men say, "Hey, that's a great video, I think you'll really enjoy it." Men go in and pretend there is no one else in the room. They want to be invisible as they look for ways to satisfy their lusts. That's because of shame. Adult bookstores are a bad place to be and they know it. Sadly, men's lust is greater than their shame, so addiction flourishes.

Satan wants us as Christian men to believe we are alone in our shame. Yet God's word assures us that what we are facing is common to man. Sure, others may have a greater struggle while some may face less of a fight. However, you are not alone.

In the following chapters we will look at how men are tempted today. My purpose is not to titillate. I want you to see that lust is not free and that it hurts others, too. Sexual addiction is *not* a victimless crime. We'll look beyond the video-enhanced images and see the real women involved in the industry of adult entertainment. Although they are called dancers, models, or stars in the adult entertainment industry, each of these women is someone's daughter, someone's child. And they are God's children, too, created in His image.

I am convinced that if Christian men would not put another cent into the porn industry, we could cripple it. That's right, cripple it. Christian men, pouring money into this destructive industry, keep it alive and flourishing. Guys, it's time for us to stop. Pornography does hurt others and we need to count the cost.

Knowing about the problem is not enough. We need a battle plan for victory. Along the way we'll take a look at some practical ideas that can help us in the fight. Some of the ideas that I'll ask you to consider will seem drastic. I hope so. At one time in my life, I needed drastic measures. If you're reading this book, perhaps you do, too. Occasional temptations that are allowed to fester and grow are no longer temptations, but sin. They become a way of life. The deeper we dig the pit, the harder it is to get out.

Before we can ever approach victory, however, we must draw near to God. As you finish this chapter, commit to reading God's word daily and claiming the victory that God promises each of us. Each chapter begins with a Bible verse. Memorize the verses so you can call on them the next time temptation calls your name. Hide God's Word in your heart (Ps. 119:11). God's Word can help us find the road to victory and avoid the path of destruction.

As you begin your journey to victory, don't forget that your temptation is common to man. Common to man, and yet God is with you every step of the way. He will provide a way of escape, and He has guaranteed ultimate victory and healing in the fullness of eternity for every battle-weary soldier who calls upon the name of the Lord Jesus Christ. In the meantime, the battle rages and the enemy has an arsenal of weapons to throw into the silent war.

2

A Defining Moment

Now flee from youthful lusts, and pursue righteousness, faith, love and peace, with those who call on the Lord from a pure heart (2 Tim. 2:22).

BEFORE WE GO ANY FURTHER, we need to get clear on a few terms. Trying to get people to agree today on what is pornography is not an easy task. Stuart Fischoff, a professor at Cailfornia State University, Los Angeles, said, "There's a fine line between erotica and pornography. Art makes it erotica."[1] Wait a minute; let me get this straight. If it's art we call it erotica and if it's not we call it pornography? Oh, now that makes sense. . . .

It's not a new battle. Pornography has been around for centuries, but the earliest obscenity case in the United States occurred in Philadelphia in 1815. Forty years after the American Revolution in a Puritan culture and we see our first case of obscenity. Times have changed in our nation's history. Today we are bombarded with obscenity issues.

The case in Philadelphia revolved around a man named

Jesse Sharpless who was found guilty of exhibiting, for money, a painting "of a man in an obscene, impudent, and indecent posture with a woman."[2] Today such a picture would probably be welcomed in magazines found in check-out lines at your local grocery store.

During the Civil War, pin-up girls became popular with soldiers on both sides of the field. A representative from the Christian Commission reported finding obscene pictures in the tents of General Grant's soldiers in 1865.[3] Pictures became available though advertisements like the one printed below in a Chattanooga newspaper:

> A very beautiful picture of the handsomest woman in the world; a peculiar rich-colored photograph in oil, taken from life; beautiful to behold. This is really a magnificent picture, a perfect gem. She is a bewitching beauty. Price fifty cents. Sent free by mail in a sealed circular envelope.[4]

Sending obscene literature through the mail became a criminal offense on the heels of the Civil War, in 1865.[5] The bill was signed by Abraham Lincoln. At the time, obscenity was defined as words or images that would trigger "sexually impure or lustful thoughts."[6] If we use that definition today, how much of what you see would be declared obscene? In 1865 this bill demanded a vote in Congress. Today a similar bill today would be laughed at on both sides of the aisle.

In 1873, Congress increased the pressure for individuals caught sending pornography though the mail. The Comstock Act passed both Houses of Congress in a debate that lasted less than an hour. The first offense was five years in prison. A second offense would bring ten years behind bars.[7] Had Hugh Hefner been born a century earlier, they would have thrown away the key to his jail cell. Instead he lives at the *Playboy* mansion.

The Supreme Court was forced to review the Comstock

Act and define obscenity in 1896. A New York publisher named Lew Rosen was convicted of publishing pictures of "females in different attitudes of indecency." An 1868 English common law case, *Regina v. Hicklin*, had defined obscenity as material "with a tendency to deprave and corrupt those whose minds are open to such immoral influences."[8] The Supreme Court in 1896 agreed. The definition was attacked in later years.

In *Roth v. United States* in 1957, the Supreme Court held that obscenity is *not* a form of expression protected by the First Amendment. Did you see the key word? *Not*. Pornographers who scream free speech need to sit down with the ACLU and read this decision together. The court also declared material obscene if "to the average person, applying contemporary community standards, the dominant theme of the material taken as a whole appeals to prurient interest." It further defined prurient interest as a "shameful or morbid interest in nudity, sex, or excretion which goes substantially beyond customary limits of candor in description or representation."[9] Wow! Shut down movie theaters, cancel cable, and say goodbye to prime-time television!

Even with defeat in 1957, pornographers did not pack up and go home. They stepped up their attack. Not surprisingly, the Supreme Court really ran into problems in the 1960s. They began to reverse lower court decisions without even giving a reason. The court's protection of minors in *Ginsberg v. New York* may have been the only redeeming obscenity decision during that turbulent decade.

Ginsberg also addressed the issue of what was considered hard-core. "No such assistance (of expert testimony) is needed by jurors in obscenity cases; indeed the 'expert witness' practices in these cases have often made a mockery out of the otherwise sound concept of expert testimony. Simply stated, hard-core pornography . . . can and does speak for itself."[10]

In 1973 the Supreme Court redefined obscenity. In *Miller v. California*, the Supreme Court once again declared that obscenity is not protected by the Constitution. It further defined obscene material with three separate elements:

1. whether the average person, applying contemporary community standards would find that the work, taken as a whole, is directed toward an unhealthy, abnormal, obsessive, morbid, or shameful interest in sex, and

2. whether the material depicts sexual conduct (ultimate sex acts, masturbation, torture, bondage, sex with animals, excretory functions, or lewd exhibition of the genitals) in a patently offensive manner substantially throughout the material, and

3. whether the work, taken as a whole, lacks serious literary, artistic, political, or scientific value.[11]

Many believe the *Miller v. California* decision successfully dealt with the confusion surrounding the definition of obscene. The case, however, was not without its critics, even on the Supreme Court. Justice Brennan led the minority for the 5-4 decision claiming that no one could produce a definition of obscenity that is not vague.[12] As the Supreme Court and our culture continue to change, it is clear that the definition of obscenity will be an issue in the 21st century.

Today, we classify pornography in two categories: hard-core and soft-core. Pornography itself is generally defined as "all sexually oriented material intended primarily to arouse the reader, viewer, or listener." The word pornography comes from two Greek words: *pornos*, which means "a harlot or prostitute and the sexual activity with such a person;" and *graphe*, which means "writing" and includes depictions and images.

In 1909 pornography was defined as "obscene or licentious writing, painting, or the like." In the 1960s pornography was no longer based on *content*, but rather on *intent*. Added to the definition were the words, "intended to arouse sexual desire." Many movies we see today would have been labeled pornographic a generation ago. Today, because of the artistic value, we take our children. Are we missing something here?

Did you notice something else? Pornography is intended to affect behavior. Some men will say they enjoy looking at pornography but are not affected by it. By its own definition, someone is being deceived.

Sociologist Diana Russell conducted a study and asked women if they had ever been upset by a man who had tried to force or persuade them "to do what they'd seen in pornographic pictures, movies, or books." Of the women surveyed, ten percent said yes. Before you raise your eyebrow at the low figure, you need to know that the "upsetting acts" included bestiality and torture.[13] We are indeed affected by pornography and so are the people closest to us.

Hard-core pornography commonly includes total nudity, lewd display of genitalia, and various kinds of sex acts. Soft-core, like *Playboy,* may have full nudity but does not emphasize violence or sexual perversion.

America has over 20,000 outlets selling *prosecutable* hard-core pornography.[14] You heard that right. Stuff that's illegal is being sold in towns across this country. There are more of these places than there are McDonald's restaurants. So how can you tell the difference between legal and illegal pornography? The secular non-partisan campaign Enough Is Enough provides the chart on the following page in their *Take Action Manual.*

What we discover is that *most* pornography is illegal according to the laws of our nation. While the last category is legal in this country, it fails in the only test relevant to the Christian man. Hold the last category up to God's word. Erotic and semi-nude pornography may be legal in the eyes of man, but it is illegal in the eyes of God.

Illegal	Illegal	Illegal	Illegal	Legal
Obscenity	Child Porno-graphy	Harmful to Minors	Broadcast Indecency	Erotic & Semi-Nude
"Hard-core" graphic material that is obsessed with sex and/or sexual violence, obviously offensive, and lacking in serious value.	Material picturing children under 18 engaged in sexual activity: primarily an underground cottage industry. It is a crime scene record of a child's sexual abuse.	Material sold or displayed to children under 18 that is unhealthy or unwhole-some, obviously not suitable, and lacking in serious value for children.	Includes messages or pictures on telephone, radio, or broadcast TV that are offensive descriptions or depictions of graphic sexual content.	"Soft-core" widely and readily available commer-cially.

As pornographers continue to push the limits of decency, you can expect the battle to rage in the future. The financial opportunity for pornographers is too great and Satan's determination to destroy the family is unrelenting. Many men are in the fight of their lives.

WORD GAMES

In our generation we have learned to play with words. The deception begins by playing with the English language. We're calling evil "good." Clubs where men go to fulfill their lust by watching women strip are called "gentlemen's clubs." Excuse me? My *American Heritage Dictionary of the English Language* defines "gentleman" as "a polite, gracious, or considerate man with high standards of propriety or correct behavior." The club and the definition have as much in common as oil and water. These clubs are no place for gentlemen.

No one wants to tell his wife he is going to a strip club. Going to a Gentlemen's Club, however, sounds prestigious. A place for male bonding. What neighborhood wouldn't want several within their border? Fat chance. Cities all across America are doing battle to rid communities of such places.

How about "adult entertainment"? It sounds like something for us to enjoy once we become of age. At 18 we get to vote and participate in adult entertainment. Could it be a rite of passage or a special moment for a father when he can finally take his son to enjoy adult entertainment? Again, the English language is being perverted.

Not only have we learned to play with words, but we have also clung to myths involving pornography. Some you may have heard before; or maybe even used in your own defense. They're called myths, however, because they are not true.

Myth #1 — *"My pornography use is about me and I'm not hurting anyone."*

Truth — A local Dallas ministry involved in the fight against pornography received an e-mail from a man who wrote, "Why do you wish to repress and severely punish fellow human creatures, simply because they don't think and act in the same way as you but *are hurting no one?*) (italics mine).

Hurting no one? Ask a wife whose self-esteem is shattered. Nothing is further from the truth. We'll learn in the next chapter that when lust is conceived, death is on the horizon. Child molesters will tell you how pornography ruined their lives and the lives of innocent children.

In her book *An Affair of the Mind* Laurie Hall wrote, "I saw my husband lose his soul to pornography. I have held other women and listened to them weep as they told me how their husbands also lost their souls to pornography. Pornography kills the soul, steals the heart, and destroys the mind. Pornography is not a victimless crime."[15] Still not convinced? Lust is sin and sin grieves the heart of God. Remember that it was sin that put Christ on the cross. Oh, we are indeed hurting someone.

Former Michigan House Judiciary Chairman Perry Bullard once vigorously defended pornography as "victimless." In 1990 he blocked efforts by local decency groups who were trying to strengthen state obscenity legislation. Bullard was later found hanging naked by a rope in his basement with sado-masochistic magazines scattered on the floor beneath him. He died of autoerotic asphyxia after engaging in a masturbatory activity using pornography to heighten sexual excitation. Victimless?[16] Hardly.

Myth #2 — *"This is an issue about morality, and you can't legislate morality."*

Truth — Who said so? *Every* law in our country is a reflection of our moral values. We legislate morality every day. Try robbing a bank. I bet you get arrested. Embezzle funds from your company. Not only will you get fired, but I bet you'll find yourself behind bars. You bet morality can be legislated. Not only does our nation legislate morality, but so does God. Look at the Ten Commandments. Sadly, we have turned the Ten Commandments into Ten Suggestions.

Myth #3 — *"God gave me this strong sexual desire."*

Truth — That's only half-right. God gave sexual desire to us . . . but mankind has perverted it. Some men are deceived into believing that sex is a need, maybe their *greatest* need. But that's not true. Sex is simply a by-product of an intimate and healthy relationship with your wife. Anything else falls short of God's design.

I had an attorney proof this chapter and he argued with me saying that sex *was* a need. I explained that air was a need, and food was a need, and water was a need, because I needed these things to survive. Without air, food, and water I will die. Take away my air and I'm dead in a few minutes. Take away my food and water and I'm dead in a few weeks.

Certainly they are needs. Not having sex, however, will not kill you. Therefore, it is not a need. My attorney friend was still not convinced but he admitted that I gave him a lot to think about.

Did you know that God tells men to stand firm? In 1 Corinthians 16:13 we are told to, "Be on the alert, *stand firm* in the faith, act like men, be strong." In the area of lust, however, He tells us to flee (2 Tim. 2:22). Do these verses conflict? No, they don't. Fleeing from lust *is* standing firm in the faith. I think it's because He knows we can't stand up against lust on our own.

But why would He tell us to flee from something that He gave us? The answer is simple. God didn't give us lust. Lust is a perversion of sexual desire, which God did give us. Sexual desire is a reason why the race continues. Our perversion of it is why families are destroyed. We need to understand the difference, for our family's sake.

Myth #4 — *"Hey, if you don't like it, don't buy it or turn it on."*

Truth - This one makes me crazy. Let's take this argument to the extreme and put hard-core movies on Saturday morning or during prime-time hours. Have erotic talk in the morning on radio stations for men on their way to work. The truth is that many God-fearing men who want to make good decisions would be tempted and many would fall. All of us sometimes need help in making good decisions. Throwing it in my face for me to turn off is not what I need. I bet you don't either. Even if we are not buying pornography, it is polluting the environment where our children are being raised.

Myth #5 — *"What about freedom of speech? This is a free country!"*

Truth — Go to a movie this weekend and in a packed theater yell, "Fire!" You'll get a fast lesson on freedom of speech. Write an article in your local newspaper and slander your neighbor. He'll help you learn more about freedom of speech, too. Pornography is not an issue of free speech. It's an issue of decency. Ridding our country of pornography does not jeopardize the First Amendment. With our rights under the First Amendment comes responsibility. Unfortunately, freedom of speech today means that we have the right to say and do anything we choose, regardless of its impact on society.

The First Amendment states that, "Congress shall make no law respecting an establishment of religion, or prohibiting the free exercise thereof; or abridging the freedom of speech, or of the press. . . ." Can anyone honestly believe that when our founding fathers penned those words that they would have included hard-core pornography? The very thought is laughable. As we saw earlier, hard-core pornography is illegal in this country. Today, the highest court in the land recognizes the cost of obscenity. It's not free.

In fact, pornography comes with a hefty price tag. Retired FBI agent William P. Kelly, who is a national consultant and lecturer on pornography, said, "Pornography and obscenity are totally destructive influences in America and must be controlled by the law." Don't try to explain to agent Kelly about the protection of pornography and freedom of speech. His 32 years of work in this area has convinced him that pornography does not need protection. It needs to be controlled.

Myth #6 — *"The solution is to make it legal and then it will go away."*

Truth — Drug addicts use the same argument. It doesn't wash. With sexual addiction, men always want more. Many men I have met started out reading *Playboy* magazine which contains nudity. The magazine satisfied them for a period of time. Eventually, they wanted more than nudity. Later magazines included pictures of various sex acts. For many men *Playboy* was a steppingstone to videos, strip clubs, adult bookstores, and much more.

Today even sadomasochism is coming into the main-stream. S&M can be described as a mixture of bondage, pain, and humiliation. Mainstream? How could something like this ever happen? Sadly, we're getting bored with sex.

"You can't watch six seconds of TV without sex . . . and its gotten to be a bore," said E. Jean Carroll, advice colum-nist for *Elle* magazine. "Our brains are foaming over with it. In order for sex to be exciting, we have to go deeper. S&M is going deeper."[17] No, pornography won't go away; it will eventually consume us.

Professor Irving Kristol said about the boredom theory, "I would like to go along with this theory but I cannot. I think it is false. The sexual pleasure one gets from pornography is autoerotic and infantile; put bluntly, it is a masturbatory exercise of the imagination when it is not masturbation pure and simple. Now, people who masturbate do not get tired of masturbation, just as sadists don't get bored with sadism and voyeurs don't get bored with voyeurism. In other words, infantile sexuality is not only a permanent temptation, it can easily become a self-reinforcing neurosis."[18]

In the fight to figure out what is obscene, we can get lost in a world of myths. Myths endure because they contain an essential element of truth. Debunking a myth involves separating the truth from the lies that are woven into it. Take the issue of freedom of speech. We would all agree that it is vital to the survival of our nation. Pornographers, however, have woven their agenda into that freedom.

Pornographers were not the first to do this. When Satan tempted Eve in the garden, he took the words that God spoke and wove in his own words. Eve could not separate the truth from the lies and she fell into sin. With pornography, we face the same dilemma. If we can separate the truth from the lies, we can destroy the myths that keep us in sin.

The war is defined in the courts, but it is fought in our minds. The Supreme Court can argue until the day the Lord returns, but the Holy Spirit within every believer reminds us of what is pure, right, lovely, of good repute, excellent, and worthy of praise (Phil. 4:8). In Washington, D.C. obscenity is colored gray. In the eyes of God the view is crystal clear.

1 "Films Draw on Nudes for Artistic Expression," *USA Today*, January 29, 1998.
2 William A. Stanmeyer, *The Seduction of Society* (Ann Arbor, MI: Servant Books, 1984), p. 94.
3 Bell I. Wiley, *The Life of Billy Yank* (New York: Doubleday & Company, Inc., 1971), p. 255.
4 Ibid., p. 256.
5 Stanmeyer, *The Seduction of Society*, p. 95.
6 "Philanthropy Culture, and Society," publication of Capital Research Center, April 1997.
7 Stanmeyer, *The Seduction of Society*, p. 95.
8 Ibid.
9 Ibid., p. 96.
10 "What Does the Law Say?" National Coalition for the Protection of Children and Families.
11 "Enough Is Enough," Take Action manual, Enough Is Enough, 1995–1996, p. 6.
12 Stanmeyer, *The Seduction of Society*, p. 104.
13 Susan Griffin, *Pornography and Silence* (New York: Harper & Row, 1981).
14 "Enough Is Enough," Take Action manual, p. 5.
15 Laurie Hall, *An Affair of the Mind* (Colorado Springs, CO: Focus on the Family Publishing, 1996), p. 68.
16 "Former Michigan House Judiciary Committee Chairman Victimized by Pornography," press release, American Family Association of Michigan, October 28, 1998.
17 E. Jean Carroll, "Sadism Going Mainstream," *American Family Association Journal*, February 1998, p. 6.
18 "Cliché Arguments," National Coalition for the Protection of Children and Families.

3

We're at War

No temptation has overtaken you but such as is common to man; and God is faithful, who will not allow you to be tempted beyond what you are able, but with the temptation will provide the way of escape also, that you may be able to endure it (1 Cor. 10:13).

I WAS LATE FOR SUNDAY SCHOOL, so I apologized to my class for keeping them waiting. I told them I had been at the mall and was heading down the escalator when all of a sudden it stopped. I explained that I was stuck on the escalator and could not get off until the repairman fixed it. My lame excuse got a good laugh and we moved on with the lesson. Obviously, no one gets stuck on a broken escalator.

As a child I use to go down escalators and try to run back up. I bet you did, too. It was easier to make it back to the top if I had not gone down too far. The farther down I went on the escalator, however, the harder it became to return to the top. Not only was the escalator still moving downward, but other people also got on, creating an obstacle.

At times it seemed hopeless and I simply gave up and allowed myself to be carried to the bottom.

In the Book of James, we learn that lust can be like my trips on the escalator. Of course, James does not use the escalator analogy, but he makes the same point.

> "But each one is tempted when he is carried away and enticed by his own lust. Then when lust has conceived, it gives birth to sin; and when sin is accomplished, it brings forth death. Do not be deceived, my beloved brethren (James 1:14–16).

Do you see how we are tempted? We are tempted when we are carried away and enticed by our own lust. Remember, however, that temptation is not a sin. The sin begins with a willful decision. It begins when we listen to our lust instead of our Lord.

Did you notice who owns the lust? It belongs to you. It belongs to me. I can't be carried away by your lust, but I can certainly be carried away by my own. As a child I was enticed to go down the escalator and try to run back up. The game is fun either direction you go — up or down. While an escalator can take you both directions, lust will *only* take you down.

In verse 15, James uses childbirth to illustrate his point. Once we are enticed by our lust, it conceives and gives birth to sin. There is no turning back in verse 15. This is our moment of willful decision where we have stepped on the escalator and we are going down. Sin has been born. We can turn back or flee from the temptation of lust, but once lust is conceived, sin is upon us.

James further tells us that when we have sinned, it brings forth death. You read that right . . . sin brings forth death. Guys, that's quite a price to pay for lust. The price is not our salvation — that is secured the moment we trust Christ as our Savior. Sin, however, does lead to death. James makes that point quite clear.

Finally, James tells us not to be deceived. That happens, doesn't it? As lust carries us away we deceive ourselves into believing that we are not hurting anyone. Sadly, death always hurts someone.

James is not talking in circles here. He's pretty clear. He does not want us to be deceived. He wants us to see the picture beyond a shadow of doubt so we won't forget it. Unfortunately, we do forget.

Too bad we don't take James at his word. How many of us have followed that same path? Maybe you've been tempted in a hotel room to watch an adult movie. You play with the remote control, flipping through channels, yet always coming back to the adult channel. After a mental debate you push the button to start the porn movie. Now you watch the movie and see women engaged in random acts of sex. Finally, through masturbation you become part of what is happening on the screen. All that's left is the feeling of shame for giving in to lust.

Lust occurs when you make a willful decision to start playing with the remote control in search of the adult channel. As you change the channel, you are filled with a sense of excitement as you are carried away more and more by your lust.

Don't forget the last part of verse 15. It brings forth death. Death? Who has ever died watching a porn movie or reading *Playboy*? What in the world is James talking about?

We'll look at a passage in the Bible where physical death took place, but is that all James is talking about? You read in the last chapter about former Michigan House Judiciary Chairman Perry Bullard, whose lust resulted in his physical death, but I'll bet you have also heard about the death of a family. I received an e-mail from a woman whose husband was spending $200-$300 a week on pornography and had repeatedly told his wife that he would stop. His promises never lasted and they later divorced.

That's the result of lust — the death of a family.

Need another example? How about the death of a testimony? Sadly, it is not uncommon to hear a scandal about a Christian leader who fell into sexual sin. Nothing destroys a congregation faster. Pastors rarely make it back to the pulpit after falling into sexual sin. That's a result of lust . . . the death of a testimony.

Still need more proof? Think about the most well-known king in the Bible, King David, the same guy who killed Goliath. The Old Testament called David a man after God's own heart. In the first chapter we learned that in 1 Corinthians 10:13 God provides a way of escape when we are tempted. See if you can identify the caution points God gives David as a way of escape.

> Then it happened in the spring, at the time when kings go out to battle, that David sent Joab and his servants with him and all Israel, and they destroyed the sons of Ammon and besieged Rabbah. But David stayed at Jerusalem (2 Sam. 11:1).

Yikes! I see a problem already. This is a time when kings go out to battle, yet where is David? He is back in Jerusalem. He is not where he is supposed to be. Men, if you want to stay out of trouble, don't be in places where you shouldn't. Here is caution point #1. David should have been with his soldiers. It gets worse for David in the next verse.

> Now when evening came David arose from his bed and walked around on the roof of the king's house, and from the roof he saw a woman bathing; and the woman was very beautiful in appearance (2 Sam. 11:2).

Aside from not being in battle, it appears that nothing wrong is going on here. Suddenly, Bathsheba comes into view of the gazing king. He is being tempted and is at a moment of decision. He has a choice, but he does not choose wisely. Did you notice the description of Bathsheba? It appears David watched her bathe long enough to know that she was very beautiful in appearance.

Noticing the bathing Bathsheba would have been a temptation to me, but if I looked long enough to notice that she was not only beautiful, but *very* beautiful, I know I would have looked too long. Lust would have been conceived. Once conceived, lust gives birth to sin. Here is caution point #2. *The woman is bathing!* Bathing women don't wear clothes. David needs to quickly look away before lust conceives sin. Not only did David look, but also he asked questions about Bathsheba.

> So David sent and inquired about the woman. And one said, "Is this not Bathsheba, the daughter of Eliam, the wife of Uriah the Hittite?" (2 Sam. 11:3).

This is both a question and a statement designed to get the attention of a king battling with lust. Wife is the key word here. Caution point #3: David has another opportunity to turn back. All he has to say is, "Did you say wife? Forget I asked the question!" David does not do that, however. David calls for her in the next verse.

> And David sent messengers and took her, and when she came to him, he lay with her; and when she had purified herself from her uncleanness, she returned to her house (2 Sam. 11:4).

When Bathsheba arrives, he has intercourse with her. As soon as the act is done, shame and guilt probably come to David. Unfortunately, it's too late. All that's left now is the cover-up.

David tries to fix his mess. He has Bathsheba's husband, Uriah, come home from the battle, hoping he will sleep with his wife. When Uriah refuses since his soldiers are still in the field, David gets him drunk. Surely in a drunken state Uriah will go home and be with his wife. No such luck. Uriah appears to be stronger drunk than David is sober. David sees no other option than to send Uriah back to the battle . . . to the front lines. The message carried back by Uriah was his own death sentence (2 Sam. 11:22–24).

Remember what happens when sin is accomplished? It brings forth death. Uriah's demise is the first death resulting from the sin of David. Notice I said first death. There is more. After the death of Uriah, David marries Bathsheba who gives birth to a son. Nathan the Prophet confronts David with his sin and declares his punishment.

> However, because by this deed you have given occasion to the enemies of the Lord to blaspheme, the child also that is born to you shall surely die (2 Sam. 12:14).

Once again we see death as a result of David's sin. David and Bathsheba's first child, an innocent child, dies. Our sin hurts the ones we love most. Death is not finished with David, however. In chapter 13, David's son Amnon rapes his half-sister Tamar. Another of David's sons, Absalom, kills Amnon for his deed. Perhaps David's sinful lust was passed on to the next generation? We can certainly make that argument here. David's family would make wonderful guests on the trashy talk shows. It's a messed-up family.

Three times God gave David a way of escape. God's opportunities to David to flee from temptation speak volumes of the wonderful patience and long suffering of God. First, David should have been with his soldiers, second, he should have fled at the sight of a bathing woman, and finally, he should have not called for her when he found out she was Uriah's wife. David and his family suffered years of pain and heartache because he was not actively looking for God's way of escape.

And don't miss an important point. While the consequences of David's sin were dire, God used the union of David and Bathsheba to later give birth to Solomon, the wisest man who ever lived. God loves us enough to even take the lowest points in our life and use them for His glory.

David is not the lone example in the Bible of problems created by lust. The mighty Samson was another. The angel of the Lord told Samson's mother that he "shall be a Nazirite to God from the womb" (Judg. 13:5). A life dedicated to God, and we see throughout his life that the spirit of God was with him. Before he defeated a lion we read that "the Spirit of the Lord came upon him mightily" (Judg. 14:6). Before he defeated 30 Philistines at Ashkelon, we read once again that "the Spirit of the Lord came upon him mightily" (Judg. 14:19). Finally, before he killed one thousand Philistines with the fresh jawbone of a donkey, we read that "the Spirit of the Lord came upon him mightily" (Judg. 15:14).

Is there any question that Samson was special? His life had a divine purpose spoken by the angel of the Lord — "he shall begin to deliver Israel from the hands of the Philistines" (Judg. 13:5). Uh-oh . . . do you see a problem with that statement? Samson will "begin" to deliver Israel. He will not be a finisher.

The text does not explain why he will only begin to deliver Israel, but we do learn something about Samson that may be the answer. The first recorded words out of his mouth give us a clue. "I saw a woman in Timnah, one of the daughters of the Philistines; now therefore, get her for me as a wife" (Judg. 14:2). In the next verse we discover that his father didn't think much of the idea (Judg. 14:3).

Not only was the marriage undesirable, but Samson ignores the counsel of his father. Why would Samson be so

foolish? The reason from Samson's mouth was simple —
"she looks good to me" (Judg. 14:3). Pornography has the
same effect on Christian men today. When we are weak,
pornography can be desirable to us, yet it's something we
need to flee from. Pornographers go to great lengths so that
we will repeat the words of Samson, "She looks good to
me."

Much like David's marriage to Bathsheba, God used
Samson's marriage to a Philistine woman for His purposes.
Later we read that Samson went to Gaza and "saw a harlot
there, and went in to her" (Judg. 16:1). His sexual appetite
for Philistine women had not subsided. Three verses later
we see the first mention of another Philistine woman, named
Delilah. Samson loved Delilah, yet later in the story Delilah
agreed to hand him over to the Philistines in exchange for
eleven hundred pieces of silver.

The lust of Samson ended with betrayal by a beautiful
woman. Men who struggle with pornography have the same
experience. When we give in to lust, we, too, will be
betrayed. Samson was betrayed because Delilah was not the
woman she claimed to be. We are betrayed because the
women in adult entertainment are not who they claim to be.
The price Samson paid was great. His loss should be a
warning for us all.

Samson lost his eyes, his family, his reputation, his
position, and finally his life. There is a cost associated with
sin. I wonder how the story of Samson would have ended if
he had counted the cost first.

The Philistines tie the blind Samson between two
pillars so he can amuse them. Samson cries out to God, "O
Lord God, please remember me and *please strengthen me
just this time, O God*, that I may at once be avenged of the
Philistines for my two eyes" (Judg. 16:28). God answered
Samson's prayer, and more Philistines died that day than he
had killed in his life. Unfortunately, Samson's life ended
that day, too.

I think I know where he failed. His prayer was too late. Would Samson have been a finisher if he had prayed, "Please strengthen me just this time, O God" as he battled lust? We'll never know. One thing I do know is that we need to pray immediately when we face sexual temptation. God knows we're weak. Ask Him for strength when you face times of weakness.

Samson's story ends with an encouraging message. While Samson is in captivity without his sight or his hair, something begins to change. As his hair grows, so does his relationship with God. Even though Samson had fallen into sin with Delilah, God did not give up on Samson. Don't be deceived into thinking that God has given up on you. God's promise is that He will *never* fail or forsake you (Josh. 1:5). God won't give up on you, and neither should you.

Unfortunately, the stories of David and Samson are being played out in many Christian homes today. While no one is watching women bathe on rooftops or revealing sacred secrets to Philistine women, we are given opportunities to give birth to sin every day.

MODERN-DAY LUST

Kevin and Carla were married for 16 years when Carla awoke one night to discover Kevin was not in bed. As she walked downstairs she heard Kevin's voice coming from the den. She peeked inside the room and saw Kevin in a chair surrounded by pornographic magazines, masturbating as he spoke to a woman on the phone. Carla backed away and ran upstairs. Later she found listings for numerous 900 numbers and phone bills totaling hundreds of dollars. Kevin and Carla were divorced three months later. Kevin's lust gave birth to sin and his marriage died.

We have discussed how we are tempted and the deadly results, but where does it begin? It begins when sin takes root in the mind. God's word tells us what we should be thinking about.

Finally, brethren, whatever is true, whatever is honorable, whatever is right, whatever is pure, whatever is lovely, whatever is of good repute, if there is any excellence and if anything worthy of praise, let your mind dwell on these things (Phil. 4:8).

That verse makes no allowance for pornography. Though we are not able to control everything that comes into our mind, we are able to choose what we do with it. I remember that at the age of ten I saw a centerfold from *Playboy* magazine. Thirty years have passed and I still remember that moment. I saw it with my eyes and it entered my mind . . . and it stuck.

"Memories of experiences that occurred at times of emotional arousal (which could include sexual arousal) get locked into the brain by an adrenal gland hormone, epinephrine, and are difficult to erase," said Dr. Victor Cline. "This may partly explain pornography's addicting effect."[1] It is amazing to me that sinful moments can get locked into the brain. Many men have told me how they remember when they were first exposed to pornography. They remember a picture or video that is captured in their memory. That was certainly the case with me. I allowed mental images to play a role in my fascination with pornographic magazines as an adolescent. Other magazines followed into adulthood.

James Allen said, "Good thoughts bear good fruit, bad thoughts bear bad fruit — and man is his own gardener."[2] Unfortunately, my life was busy producing bad fruit.

I met with a Christian man named Thomas who said his greatest temptation is peep shows at adult theaters. He spends quarter after quarter watching short "films" in a tiny booth and can't even guess the amount of money he has spent in the past year. Adult theaters are never his first thought, however. His lust can begin by reading the Sunday newspaper and seeing a lingerie ad. Like King David, Thomas looks long enough at the display of nearly nude women to know that they are very beautiful. His lustful thoughts are allowed to grow. Before the day is over, he may end up at the adult theater feeding a booth with quarters.

I do not face the same temptation as Thomas. The reason is simple. I have never exposed myself to adult theaters. Other men struggle with phone sex because they allowed themselves to try it once. For some, that's all it takes. Satan can take that one exposure, which *we* allowed to take root, and feed it. The more you are exposed to adult entertainment, the stronger the temptation becomes.

Have you figured out the key? Be careful what you're exposed to. Unfortunately, in our culture today, we sometimes don't get a choice. If you're reading this book you are probably fighting a battle with sexual temptation. Like many men, you may be going though an addictive cycle, lost in a sense of hopelessness.

Step One —— Volunteering for the Addiction

Since addiction to pornography and adult entertainment is a battle, I have put the addictive cycle into military terms. It begins with volunteering for the addiction. That's right, this is an all-volunteer addiction. Someone else may have exposed you to pornography, but the addiction belongs to you. Exposure is the first step in the addictive cycle and understanding it is also the first key to victory. We need to take responsibility for our sin. Most of us volunteer as children when we are first exposed to pornographic material, but enlistment doesn't have to be for a lifetime.

"I can remember feeling both deep guilt and excitement as I leafed through the pages," Michael said as he remembered the day he found pornography in his father's closet. "Somehow I knew it was wrong for me to be looking at such pictures, but curiosity and fascination overcame my misgivings."[3]

Michael is certainly not alone. When Carl entered his

first topless club, he was overcome with excitement. "The eye-popping spectacle of this gorgeous woman baring all and jiggling it in front of me, and the boisterous spirit of the all-male audience combined to overpower me. I walked out of the bar two hours later feeling strangely warmed, intensely excited."[4]

The addiction is all about lust. Understanding the power of lust is important as we fight the addiction. Frederick Buechner in *Godric* said, "Lust is the ape that gibbers in our loins. Tame him as we will by day, he rages all the wilder in our dreams by night. Just when we think we're safe from him, he raises up his ugly head and smirks, and there's no river in the world flows cold and strong enough to strike him down. Almighty God, why dost thou deck men out with such a loathsome toy?"[5]

That's the power of lust. It never satisfies and always leaves you wanting more. As Christian men we understand the power, and hate what it's doing, yet we have great difficulty getting beyond its reach.

I love how Chuck Swindoll described lust:

> Lust is no respecter of persons. Whether by savage assault or subtle suggestion, the minds of a wide range of people are vulnerable to its attack: sharp professional men and women, homemakers, students, carpenters, artists, musicians, pilots, bankers, senators, plumbers, promoters, and preachers as well. Its alluring voice can infiltrate the most intelligent mind and cause its victim to believe its lies and respond to its appeal.

> And beware: It never gives up; it never runs out of ideas. Bolt your front door, and it will rattle at the bedroom window, crawl into the living room through the TV screen, or wink at you out of a magazine in the den.[6]

When you expose yourself to pornography, Satan is able to use lust get a toehold in your life. Continued exposure leads to a foothold. Finally, Satan has you trapped when a stronghold has been established. Unfortunately, a stronghold needs constant feeding. Your lust provides an appetizing menu that promises to satisfy.

I remember my days in the military. Soldiers complained about everything from the work to the hours to the food, but many re-enlisted when it was time. Christian men struggling with pornography do the same thing. We complain about our struggle, yet we always seem to go back for more. That's the power of Satan's stronghold.

Step Two —— Search & Destroy

Overcome with temptation, men search for satisfaction. Satisfaction may be a magazine, video, telephone call, visit to a strip club, or perhaps the hiring of a prostitute. Whatever the end result, it takes a "search and destroy" mission to find it. Why do I call this a "search and destroy" mission? Because the Christian man knows while he is searching, he has already been defeated. Sadly, in our culture today, our search never lasts very long. The object of our lust is found too easily with no visible risk.

While we are searching we begin to rationalize our actions. What rationalizations have you used in the past? Here are a few that our society today offers, though none would get the approval of a holy and righteous God.

- Pornography is art. It's funded by the U.S. government, so why should we deny ourselves?" I would much rather use the Bible for determining what I should and should not expose myself to. The U.S. government and the National Endowment for the Arts have had some strange ideas about the definition of "art."

- Why would God want us to be ashamed of looking at the beauty He created? There is nothing unnatural about nudity." Beauty is wonderful. Several women in the Bible are described as being "beautiful of form and face." When our admiration of beauty turns into lust, we have crossed the line.

- I enjoy the articles!" I remember hearing this one in college. Yes, *Playboy* had great articles, but if you're looking for something good to read, go to the library.

- Pornography will help my sex life. It will help keep my sex life fresh and exciting. And when my wife is not in the mood, I won't have to burden her since I have my pornography. I'm really doing it for her." If you are doing it for her, then I suppose you don't have any problem telling her all about it. I doubt after hearing your rationalization will your wife say, "Gee, you sure do love me!" The tears you see won't be tears of joy.

The most powerful rebuttal of this rationalization comes from the words of a wife: "Pornography didn't turn my husband into a great lover. Far from being the sexual liberator it purports to be, pornography enslaves participants in sexual activities that destroy their personhood. Far from being the ticket to endless rounds of sexual highs, pornography introduces a strain into relationships that squashes sexual enjoyment. As far as I'm concerned, pornography gets an "F" in sex education."[7]

- "Sure I look at pornography, but there are a whole bunch of folks who are doing things a lot worse. And who among us is really pure anyway?" That's funny. When our children use the "everyone is doing it" argument, we usually fuss at them.

- "These are just lingerie ads in my daily newspaper. This isn't pornography!" Certainly, lingerie ads are not defined as pornographic. What do men think about though as they gaze at the ads? Are the thoughts

lovely, pure and righteous according to Philippians
4:8? I've seen a lot of lingerie ads in my day. If I look
too long, my thoughts turn to lust.

- "Sure I look at pornography, but it does not involve
  actual contact with a woman." The definition of lust is
  not limited to actual contact with women. Computer-
  enhanced women work quite well, too.

- "Sometimes I just need a release (before, during, after)
  a busy week. It's not like it's an addiction." Alcoholics
  use the same argument. It doesn't work.

At some time in our life, all of us have rationalized sin.
I recently met a seminary student who not only rationalized
his sin, he tried to turn it into a ministry! Patrick worked as
a bouncer at a sexually oriented business. At the end of the
evening many of the women were battling with self-esteem
issues so he "ministered" to them as he walked them to their
car. After listening to his story I told him I had a few
questions for him.

"Patrick, how many women have you led out of the
industry?" I inquired.

"None," he replied.

"Well then," I asked, "how many have you led to
Christ?"

"None, but it takes time to get to know them and build
relationships," he implored.

"Patrick," I said, looking him squarely in the face,
"you're 'ministry' isn't working. It's broken. It doesn't have
the appearance of evil, it *is* evil. Today is your last day with
that 'ministry.' " My time with Patrick was another reminder to me about the power of sexual addiction and the
deception of Satan. It's a one-two punch that is knocking
Christian men out cold. Our only hope for victory is to be
close to Jesus so He can step in before another one of Satan's
punches hits its mark.

Step Three —— D-Day

D-Day follows our "search and destroy" mission. In World War II, D-Day was a day of great victory. In the addictive cycle, the victory is hollow. For a moment we are filled with an incredible sense of excitement and sexual release, having captured the object of our lust. "Victory" is ours! D-Day ends with orgasm, through masturbation or even intercourse. The true victory of D-Day belongs to Satan with deception, defeat, discouragement, and disgust.

Step Four —— Defeat and Occupation

In the battle of sexual temptation, D-Day brings defeat in the arms of guilt and shame. Our momentary pleasure and excitement are swept away. Shame is so great that sin is not confessed to God, as if we can somehow hide it from Him. It's shame and guilt that lead to a feeling of hopelessness. Shame is a hemorrhage of the soul and a silent killer much like blood pressure is a symptom-free destroyer.

God will not allow the Christian man to give into lust without a feeling of shame. "For the flesh sets its desire against the Spirit, and the Spirit against the flesh; for these are in opposition to one another, so that you may not be able to do the things you please" (Gal. 5:17).

Shame. Surely God cannot forgive you *again* for committing the same sexual sin for which you've asked forgiveness countless times before. You're defeated and ready to enter the next step of the vicious cycle.

It is important to remember, however, that continued sin will reduce the shame a Christian man feels. In 1 Thessalonians 5:19 it is written, "Do not quench the Spirit." How do we quench the Spirit? By refusing to listen to the Holy Spirit. We quench the Spirit when we take matters into our own hands. By continuing to make bad choices, we are certainly quenching the Spirit. The irony is that the shame will eventually end for the Christian man, either through victory or utter defeat.

Michael thought about seeing a counselor about his fascination with pornography, "but I felt too ashamed and frightened. What was happening inside me was terrifying, but I kept the dark secret to myself."[8] Guys, when we keep our shame to ourselves, fearful of talking to others or to God himself, the enemy is occupying territory that you need to surrender to God. And secret sin and shame are vulnerable points from which the enemy launches the next skirmish for your soul. There will always be another lingerie ad, another lonely night on the road, another pornographic magazine in the convenience store. Can the battle end? Can the war be won? We resolve to be strong, to use self-control. We feel confident.

Step Five —— Treaty or Cease-fire?

Time seems to be a healer as we finally take our shame and guilt before the Father. Our wounds appear to be healed as we experience a renewed strength to be strong the next time. A treaty is offered in the form of our promises to God to fight the good fight. Battle plans for victory are set in motion. Our temptation leaves, but just for a season. What we call a treaty, Satan calls a cease-fire. We can be sure he will attack again, when we are facing weak moments.

Step Six —— Escalation

Satan hates the confession and repentance of a godly man. He hates defeat and will attack once again with greater force, knowing where you are weak. After Jesus was victorious following the third temptation recorded in Luke 4, we see Satan's plan in verse 13.

> And when the devil had finished every temptation, he departed from Him until an opportune time (Luke 4:13).

Imagine that! Satan will strategically wait for an opportune time to attack again. When he finds the right moment, the cease-fire is over. His desire is to send you on another "search and destroy" mission . . . and the battle continues. Trapped in the destructive cycle, men can sometimes feel unable to control their lustful thoughts, even though they know it is harmful.

One prominent leader of a Christian ministry was successful at resisting most lures to pornography. When he traveled, however, he would find himself surfing cable channels for porn.

"I'd tell myself, at least I'm not going to peep shows or X-rated movies," he said. Yet when he watched television porn, he was "filled with guilt and condemnation. I hated it; I was sick of my sin. But I couldn't break away."[9]

You can't change what you have been exposed to. You can, however, refrain from exposing yourself to anything new. In a survey I conducted with over 100 Christian men, all of them said the first pornography they saw was in a magazine. (I believe many in the next generation will find their first exposure on the Internet, thanks to the service many families pay for each month.)

What I have discovered in talking to men is that we may start with magazines, but soon our appetite requires something more. *Playboy* no longer completely satisfies our lusts. We need more — in frequency, intensity, and variety. Soft-core pornography leads to hard-core pornography. It becomes an addiction much like drugs and alcohol. We need more to achieve the same level of "high."

TWO EXTREMES —— MIKE AND TED

Certainly there are exceptions. When I met with Mike he explained that he had been a frequent reader of *Playboy* magazine. One day while he was reading he realized something important. He realized his wife would never look like the airbrushed woman in the magazine. He threw the magazine away and never picked up another one. Mike is one extreme.

Ted is the other extreme. I bet you know Ted. His last name was Bundy. In January 1988, serial killer Ted Bundy was executed in Florida for the brutal murder, rape, and dismemberment of at least 28 women and girls from Utah, Washington, Idaho, Colorado, and Florida. In an interview with James Dobson from Focus on the Family, Bundy said his desire to kill was fueled by pornography.

He grew up in a loving Christian home but began reading soft-core pornography when he was 12 or 13 years old. "From time to time we would come across pornographic books of a harder nature . . . a more graphic, explicit nature than we would encounter at the local grocery store," said Bundy in the James Dobson interview the day before he was executed.

Bundy knew well the effects of the pornography addiction. "It happens in stages," he said. His exposure kept him looking for something more potent with a greater sense of excitement. Sadly, he was out of control. "Something snapped and I knew I couldn't control it anymore," Bundy admitted.

He also knew his death would not end such murders. "We are your sons and we are your husbands," warned Bundy. "And we grew up in regular families and pornography can reach out and snatch a kid out of any house today."

During his time in prison Bundy learned the harm of pornography. "I've met a lot of men who were motivated to commit violence just like me and without exception, every one of them was deeply involved in pornography."

As horrible as his crimes were, Ted Bundy knew the irony of our culture today. "Well-meaning, decent people will condemn behavior of a Ted Bundy while they're walking past a magazine rack full of the very kinds of things that send a young kid down the road to be Ted Bundy's."[10]

Mike is at one end and Ted Bundy is at the other. These two men are the extremes. The rest of us are somewhere in the middle. My question for you is, what direction are you going? With God's help, you can be free.

It won't be easy. Years ago men had to go to seedy parts of town to find pornography. Not so today. From my home I can drive to several places that sell magazines and videos in less than five minutes.

THE FROG IN THE KETTLE

The horror of pornography and adult entertainment has slowly permeated our culture. The destruction can be compared to the frog in the kettle. Thrown into a kettle of boiling water, the frog will quickly try to escape. Throw a frog into cool water set on boil and the frog will soon die unknowingly. Those who probably know best about the change in our culture are the ones who left the country for an extended period.

Following his return from Vietnam after eight years in a POW camp, Admiral Jeremiah Denton was shocked at what he saw. "I had been familiar with downtown Norfolk from 1943 to 1965. . . . A few houses of ill repute were sprinkled about in the Navy town," said Denton. "But it was normal enough. But new to my eyes were block after block of tawdry looking massage parlors. It was about two o'clock in the morning and they were all closed, but the titles were there. There were X-rated movies and sex-oriented shops. I had to ask Jane (his wife) what "massage parlor" and "X-rated" meant. Over the next few months, I was to absorb the whole picture of how far our country had strayed from its moorings during the time I was gone."[11]

Try to imagine the days of your parents and grandparents. How would they have responded to television shows like "Dawson's Creek," or restaurants like Hooters? How about radio programs like Howard Stern or catalogs like Victoria's Secret? Trust me, there would have been a public outcry. Today, that voice is almost silent. Our culture has changed, and what was once beyond comprehension has now become socially acceptable.

"We have become so legitimate that it's unbelievable," boasted Jim South, who owns an adult modeling agency in Sherman Oaks, California.[12] Unfortunately, South is correct. And in the midst of this moral sewage, Christian men are expected to live in a manner pleasing to our Lord. That challenge is more difficult today than it has ever been. It will be even tougher for our sons.

CHASED BY TEMPTATION

Part of the problem is that the search for adult entertainment is so easy. Not only is the search easy, but I believe today our temptation chases us. You heard that right. Sexual temptation is thrown in our face. I remember in the movie *Jaws*, how the shark hunters were aghast when the shark began to chase them as they tried to escape. Sexual temptation does the same thing today. Go to a convenience store to buy a gallon of milk and you have to deal with the temptation of a magazine rack. Go to a video store to rent a family movie and you have to deal with the temptation of the back room filled with adult videos. Drive down the road past billboards for strip clubs and you have to deal with the temptation of a reclining, scantily clad woman on the billboard. Walk into a motel room while you are away from your family and you have to deal with the temptation of turning on an adult movie. It seems to have no end.

One Sunday morning I was sitting at the breakfast table looking at a department store insert in the *Dallas Morning News* when I came across the underwear section. I showed my wife, who was sitting across from me, something interesting. The men's underwear was pictured neatly packaged in a plastic wrapper. On the package I read that the underwear provided "comfort I could feel." The women's underwear, however, was not in a wrapper, but was worn by a beautiful model. Do women really need to see their underwear on a beautiful model to make a decision on whether to buy it? I don't think so. I bet women would do fine seeing it in a plastic wrapper, too. Unfortunately, we have to be alert even reading the Sunday paper where many men have told me they struggle with lingerie ads.

I had another reminder of temptation's chase when I took a day off to write. I had just written about how we are chased by temptation when my wife asked me to take our teenage daughter to school. Of course I agreed and enjoyed the time with her. On my way home I stopped at a convenience store to pick up a Dr. Pepper for my wife. Walking towards the store, I heard the pay phone ring. I don't know why, but when I hear a phone ring, I think someone needs to answer it. I was the only one close. The guy on the other end sounded very friendly. He said someone calling from that number had paged him. He asked questions about who might have called and I answered them politely. Then he explained he and his wife were new in the area and were looking for another man to have sex with them. He gave me all the sordid details and asked if I would consider the offer. I was dumbfounded. I should have hung up, but I didn't. I don't know if this was a crank call or if he was serious. It didn't matter because I was not tempted. What did happen was that thoughts entered my mind that I had to deal with. Hanging up right away would have been a better choice.

Instead I heard him out and said, "My friend, you need Jesus." My new friend hung up on me. When I got home I told my wife and said, "I don't need this!" The experience was another reminder to me that we are surrounded by sex today. My chance conversation with an anonymous stranger stayed with me for several days.

We are certainly bombarded with sexual messages today. Someone once said that temptation, unlike opportunities, will always give you a second chance. Sadly, our culture today gives us third and fourth chances, too. Guys, it's everywhere. Is it possible to make it through a prime-time TV show without a sexual situation or innuendo being thrown at you? For some men, one such situation can send them off on a "search and destroy" mission.

However, we can take God at His word and believe that what we're facing is common to man. In an informal survey, every man said he had been exposed to pornography. At some point in our young lives, curiosity got the best of us. While some men have dealt with their exposure and do not struggle with sexual temptation, many others are feeling defeated.

As for the strength of the temptation, only 18 percent of the respondents to my survey said their temptation was weak. While 63 percent said their temptation was mild, 19 percent of these Christian men said it was strong or overpowering. You may be surprised to learn that 82 percent of us are fighting some kind of battle, but for almost one out of every five Christian men, the battle is horrific.

According to the Maryland Coalition Against Pornography (MCAP), 40 to 60 percent of Christian men are involved with pornography in some way.[13] Sadly, it's a battle many men fight alone, too ashamed to tell anyone else.

Remember, being tempted is not a sin. Giving in to the temptation, however, certainly is a sin. Of the respondents to my survey, 57 percent said they have viewed pornography in the past year. Over half, including many of those who said their temptation was mild, are losing the battle of sexual temptation. Imagine the blow we could deliver to this horrible industry if Christian men could find a way of escape.

Well, you know the problem, but don't lose hope. We may be at war, but there is a path to victory. And Jesus has cleared the way.

 1 Victor Cline, *Pornography's Effects on Adults & Children* (New York: Morality in Medica, Inc.), p. 7.
 2 Bruce H. Wilkinson, editor, *Victory Over Temptation* (Eugene, OR: Harvest House Publishers, 1998), p. 168.

3 Becky Beane, "The Problem of Pornography," *Jubilee Magazine*, Summer 1998, p. 17.

4 "The War Within," *Leadership/92*, Fall Quarter 1992, p. 98.

5 Frederick Buechner, *Godric* (New York: Atheneum, 1980).

6 Bruce H. Wilkinson, *Victory over Temptation* (Eugene, OR: Harvest House Publishers, Inc., 1998), p. 217.

7 Laurie Hall, *An Affair of the Mind* (Colorado Springs, CO: Focus on the Family Publishing, 1996), p. 86.

8 Beane, "The Problem of Pornography," p. 18.

9 Ibid.

10 *Fatal Addiction*, Focus on the Family Films, 1989.

11 "Philanthropy Culture & Society," publication of Capital Research Center, April 1997, p. 7–8.

12 "An Uneasy Peace? Valley's Porn Industry Thrives — Quietly," *Los Angeles Daily News*, March 29, 1998.

13 Maryland Coalition Against Pornography, Silver Spring, Maryland, November 1997.

4

She Has a Name

But put on the Lord Jesus Christ, and make no provision for the flesh in regard to its lust (Rom. 13:14).

ARE YOU READY FOR A NEWS FLASH? Naked women are beautiful. Really. Picture this scenario. Fly a group of men up to the most beautiful site at Denali State Park in Alaska. Point them all to a magnificent snowcapped mountain, with caribou and brown bears off in the distance. The gushing river is flowing below with white-capped waves. Listen to them "ooh" and "aah" at the majestic beauty of this scene. Then have a woman walk by naked. Without exception, every eye will move from the creation to the creature. It will happen in an instant. She will have their undivided attention . . . because she is naked.

How about this scenario? It's the bottom of the ninth in the seventh game of the World Series. The home team is down by three runs and has two outs with the bases loaded. The home-run king is at the plate with a three-two count. His two strikes were towering foul balls that brought the crowd to its feet. The pitcher looks for a sign and nods his head. To your surprise, the woman two rows in front of you pulls off her top. Suddenly the game no longer matters.

Women are beautiful to us because God made them that way. Their beauty and our desire are God-given. The nakedness of a woman has a powerful impact on us. For you married men, do you remember the first time you saw your wife naked? What a sight to behold! Everything about her was incredible. But along the way, something happened. The thrill of seeing *her* naked ended. I suspect your wife no longer has that power because you have seen her all your married life. What captures you now is the nakedness of *another* woman. For many men it is the forbidden fruit of women found in the adult entertainment industry.

I've seen many women involved in the adult entertainment industry. Some performed onstage and danced in smoky clubs packed full of men. Others were in movies and videos. Like anyone else who has ever watched trashy talk shows, I have seen strippers and porn stars talk about their involvement in the industry. Of course, women who have graced the pages of adult magazines have not escaped my view either. All of these women had one thing in common. They appeared to enjoy their work. On one talk show the women spoke about the amount of money they made which was mind-boggling. One porn star not only talked about the money, she bragged about the "family feeling" provided in the world of porn. They took care of each other. She could not imagine doing anything else. There is one other thing you need to know about these women. I never cared to know their names.

It is easy to dehumanize women in adult entertainment. Their reason for existence is to satisfy lust. Nothing more. Their names are insignificant. A former political consultant who was forced to resign after a sordid affair with an expensive prostitute said on the "Oprah Winfrey Show" that he didn't see a hooker as a person. She was a possession without thoughts or a life of her own. I always thought my lust was about me and didn't hurt anyone else, certainly not the women who profited from my lust. We used each other and no one got hurt, or so I believed.

Today I know the truth. I know about the drugs and alcohol and the abuse. Everything I thought I knew about this industry was based on deception. Pornographers want us to believe that no one is getting hurt. Nothing could be further from the truth. I had the opportunity to interview women who escaped the adult entertainment industry. As I got to know them by name, their stories left a permanent imprint on my heart.

I learned that there is a cost for lust. Every cent I spent on pornography and adult entertainment was used to keep these women trapped in a world where they were dehumanized, where their value was based on their beauty and their willingness to participate in degrading sexual activities. Those who claim to love them as "family" have perverted the word and betrayed them. Tragically, the family in the world of adult entertainment is about use and abuse.

Women in adult entertainment have real names and I want to introduce you to a few of them. In Isaiah 49:16, it is written, "Behold, I have inscribed you on the palms of My hands." Their names are significant to God and I hope you and I never forget them. I hope you remember each one when you are tempted by lust. I pray that you count the cost they pay for your sexual pleasure. I want it written on my heart that lust for them grieves the heart of God.

ELISE

I hurt after speaking to Elise. Abuse 30 years earlier still brought her to tears. Her father became involved with pornographers and when she was five years old he sold his only daughter into the ugly world of porn. For four years Elise was involved in the most heinous types of sexual sin. She spoke of sadomasochism, brutality, and bestiality. Before she was nine she witnessed the filming and death of a little girl caused by rough sex with a man. She called it a "snuff" film.

At the age of ten the abuse stopped, only to start again six years later at the pleading of her father whose debt threatened his life. "In order to protect my Dad, I would do anything," she said.

Elise was flown in a private jet from Illinois to a large estate in Miami for weekends of sex with wealthy and affluent men. In a room at the estate Elise would have sex with numerous men. The sex was often filmed and the tape was given to the men. On Monday she was flown home. She never knew when the next call would come.

Elise was lavished with beautiful gowns and expensive jewels. She was fed like royalty. Her "princess" treatment was based solely on her sexual performance and cooperation. She and other young girls she knew lived a life full of fear and threats. On one occasion when a girl openly protested the sexual abuse, the men who operated the business led her and the other girls out to the swimming pool.

"They threw her in the pool as we watched and the shooting practice began," she said. The girl was murdered before their eyes for her failure to cooperate. "I would rather have died than go on living," Elise said. "Death is what had value." If Elise or the other girls disagreed or refused to submit to the desires of these men, they were punished. She said the pornographers had her complete cooperation.

"I didn't want to get to know the other girls because I never knew what would happen to them," Elise explained. She was cast to perform in hard-core videos for pornographers to sell. She remembers the costumes and big white sets where the filming took place. During some video shoots she was tied up and beaten.

The trips to Miami for weekends of sex ended at the age of 20. Shortly afterwards she was married but her life in the world of porn did not end. Her husband ran with a fast crowd and his best friend got Elise involved in print pornography without her husband's knowledge.

"I did that for a year and didn't see anything wrong with it. It was the most mild of all pornography that I had been involved with," Elise claimed. "Women do not have a value of who they are. I was taught that my only value was my body."

I asked Elise about the women involved in the industry. She said she wonders how many of the girls she worked with are still alive. Drugs and alcohol are rampant. "If a woman gets in it, they have to take drugs and alcohol to obliterate the feeling that this is wrong," she said.

All she saw in the men was their selfishness. "These are men who need to satisfy themselves no matter what the expense," she cried. "It didn't matter if it destroyed children's lives. It didn't matter if it destroyed women's lives." She only saw the sexual addiction as a way for men to avoid intimacy.

Elise's involvement in the world of porn left her family in ruins. Her father is dead and her mother committed suicide. Her brother's family is in shambles as he is trapped in sexual addiction. Her own marriage experienced years of hardship.

"I still struggle with intimacy and trust," Elise said. "I may never have the sexual intimacy God designed. I was robbed. It almost destroyed my children. The hell they went through causes me my greatest grief." As she spoke, her tears were unstoppable. It has even affected her relationship with God. "If I move into intimacy with God, I can't seem to stay there because I get too afraid," she said.

I spoke with Elise a second time a week later and she admitted she had had a bad week. Our conversation had brought back a flood of painful memories that she had to deal with once again. As I looked into her eyes, I regretted conducting the interview because of the pain it had caused.

Of all of the stories I heard, this one hurt most since I

knew Elise more than the other women. As much as her story grieved me, I knew she was not alone. There are many other women who could tell the same tragic story. And they have names, too.

STEFANI

I asked a female coworker to accompany me to meet with Stefani, whose name I had gotten from Dan Panetti at the Dallas Association for Decency. Stefani and I had talked several times on the phone and she had given a good description of herself so I spotted her easily in the restaurant. Extremely attractive with short blond hair, she looked more like the girl next door than a topless dancer.

Stefani had not dreamed of a dancing or modeling career. Growing up in a loving Christian family, she claimed that she had no dysfunction in her past that would lead to topless dancing. All she wanted to do was make ends meet. When Stefani lost her job, a friend suggested she try being a waitress at the topless club where she worked. Since Stefani needed money badly, she decided to try it on a short-term basis until she could get back on her feet.

After one week as a waitress she was approached about dancing. Waitresses pull in a few hundred a night while the dancers were making over $1,000 on a good night. Stefani explained that 90 percent of the dancers start out as wait-resses. Most were single moms with children.

"I was treated really well. The club owners took me shopping and since I was about to be evicted, they took care of my bills," Stefani explained. She was given a tennis bracelet, roses, a CD player, a mink coat, and $6,500 breast implants. "The owners told me they were my best friends. Many of the dancers need a family and love, someone who cares for them," Stefani said. "When dancers would call in saying they were too tired to come in, they were told not to worry about it. The club would get them a pedicure and manicure instead."

The owners of the club liked Stefani because she had the wholesome look that was attractive to men. She was given more attention than many of the other dancers. In addition to her appearance, the owners liked the fact that Stefani was very bright. The club provided Stefani a trainer to help keep her in shape. As promised, the money was great. Stefani had to work only four days a month to pay all her bills.

As Stefani became a part of her new "family," she realized she was pulling away from her friends and family. "Friends would call me and ask if I was still alive," she said. "All the friends you use to have you don't talk to anymore." She would lie to them and avoid staying in touch.

I was surprised when Stefani told me that the club did not pay her. It was just the opposite; she had to pay the club to dance. In addition to paying the club she had to tip the valet $20, the DJ $50, the floor men $20, and the house mom about $80. The house mom doted on the dancers, taking care of their every need from hair spray to food. All of Stefani's money came from the men who entered the club.

With over 100 dancers employed by the club, the girls got onstage for one set of three songs each evening. The dancers picked the songs. The big money was in "table dancing" where dancers walked up to tables and asked men if they would like them to dance for them. Men paid dancers one to five dollars for dancing onstage. Table dancing, however, brought a steady flow of twenties.

When dancers wanted to buy a car or a house, the club would give them fake paystubs and a fake W-2 listing them as a public relations manager at the club. Whatever the dancers needed, the club owners tried to provide.

Stefani also got offers from other clubs. Owners in other states would come down and invite girls to work at their clubs where they might be featured as "Miss Nude Texas," a title that was never earned.

"They would pay for food, hotel, and plane fare. I could

also tell them that I would have bills due and they would take care of those, too," Stefani said. "In addition to paying my bills and the tips, clubs would offer $15,000 to take the job."

There was other solicitation. Dancers were asked to star in porn movies on occasion. "We were told that these were foreign movies and would never be seen in the U.S.," she said. While Stefani never took them up on the offer, it would have paid her over $15,000 if she had. Other offers included several thousand dollars for web pages on the Internet. Magazine offers were common, too.

In spite of all the money and attention, Stefani hated dancing. She would work a few days and go home and cry. "It affected my life horribly," she said. "You don't put yourself in an environment where you would interact with people." Her self-esteem was shattered.

Leaving the "family" was hard since the club harassed dancers who tried. Phone calls, visits to the home, and threats of telling their family or new employer were commonplace. Stefani changed her address and appearance in an effort to hide.

Stefani loathed the men. "We hated them. You act like you like them," Stefani explained. "Men would say the most disgusting things to me that I would remember. I felt horrible. We had no respect for married men who came in here to watch us. It's not harmless fun. It's a bad place for men to be. It makes women feel horrible about themselves." As Stefani spoke each word her voice got louder and the words came faster. Suddenly, in a crowded restaurant, she burst into tears. I put my pen down as the woman I brought consoled Stefani and patted her arm. Even after months out of the business, her wounds were still fresh. I ended the interview and we turned to small talk.

Driving back to the office, my friend and I agreed that we were emotionally exhausted. I hurt for Stefani, yet was thankful that she seemed to be out for good. Later that day my boss asked me how the interview went and my emotions caught up with me. As my eyes welled up with tears, I could not speak. In my past I had seen many dancers like Stefani. It finally hurt me to see one, because this one I knew by name.

AMY

It was a cloudy, rainy afternoon in Dallas when another female coworker and I met Amy for lunch. The restaurant was Amy's choosing so she led us to the back of the building. The side room we entered was dimly lit as we seated ourselves in a booth. I had 15 prepared questions to ask Amy. After she finished answering the first, I looked at my watch and saw that over 30 minutes had past. With one question Amy instantly became transparent to two strangers. Her 30-minute answer to the first question was filled with more pain than most people experience in a lifetime.

Amy is in her early thirties. As she spoke I noticed something about her eyes. Of course, she was very beautiful, yet with Amy there was something more than her looks. As the interview began, I wasn't sure what it was.

She grew up surrounded by poverty in a home void of love. Her mother, married six times, was physically abusive to Amy. Once when Amy was getting something out of the refrigerator, she dropped a jar of olives on the floor. Filled with anger, her mother pushed her head to the floor and forced Amy to eat every olive that had spilled.

Beginning at age four, a stepfather sexually abused her for three years. Her alcoholic mother later gave Amy the responsibility for caring for her siblings. Unwilling and unprepared to accept such responsibility, Amy rebelled.

"I felt completely alone and hated by my parents," Amy said. With a shattered self-esteem, Amy turned to drugs and alcohol at the age of 12. The abuse from her mother continued through her teenage years and at the age of 18 a friend suggested she try dancing at a local strip club. Amy showed up at the club and danced that night.

Her first night was horrible. "I had to drink a lot that first night to make it through," she claimed. Not only was she inexperienced at dancing, but her opinion of her appearance was low. Making little money, her first night dancing was her last for over a year. Amy left the club and moved to the excitement of California. While she was dancing at a club outside Los Angeles she hit rock bottom. She almost died after a bad experience smoking crack. She returned to Texas but her mother discouraged care at a treatment center. Amy tried to take care of the problem on her own surrounded by people who drank and took drugs. She failed.

Amy found a job as a bartender at a country-western bar but was fired for drinking too much. Struggling financially and lost in her drug and alcohol addiction, she began dancing again at one of the nastiest clubs in Dallas, but this time it was different. Fearing she would kill herself, she cleaned herself up and quit the drugs and alcohol in October 1991. She hoped to make enough money in a year to quit dancing for good. She poured herself into the business and had cosmetic surgery. With a new look and new attitude, Amy was soon making over $400 a night. She landed jobs as a featured dancer, making a base salary up to $3,000 a week plus tips and expenses. She declined offers to do porn movies and magazines that followed.

In her first relationship after getting sober she tasted true intimacy, but she hated relying on that person financially. She left the relationship after two years, knowing it was not right and she quit dancing. Amazingly, she got a job as a nanny. Her childcare days were short-lived so she returned once again to what she did best — dancing.

Moving again, this time to Florida, she earned $1,000 nightly dancing completely nude at a Fantasy Fair. "Hustling was the name of the game and I had it all figured out," she said. "Every time men walked in the door I made them feel unique."

Her success gave her a false sense of self-esteem.

"While I was on the stage I felt famous," she said. Still, there was a deep void in her life.

"On the way to the gym one day I remember asking God to get me out," she said. No matter how she looked or how much she made, Amy knew her life was off track.

She met an Australian man in a club and returned to Australia with him where she posed for *Penthouse* of Australia. After seeing the explicit pictures of herself, she told him not to send the pictures in.

"Somewhere in my heart I knew it was not right," she said. She began taking medication for depression yet when she returned to America, Amy began working at two clubs and developed quite a following of men. When she danced this time it hurt her to see girls do obscene things for money.

"My soul was aching," Amy claimed. She began dating a man from the club. While they were dating he made it clear that he did not want Amy dancing any longer. "We were fighting all the time," she said. "And he drank too much." Her boyfriend grew up in a Christian home so they started attending church together to see if they could find the answer to their problems.

"The Holy Spirit was yelling at me," Amy said. "Something really happy was growing inside me, but I knew I had been so bad." She got involved in church and began discipling with an older woman.

"I soon found out the Holy Spirit was working within me," she said. One evening she walked into the smoky club to dance and saw clearly what was happening. "It was keeping me there and I was trapped." Faced with large bills, she knew it would be hard, if not impossible, to make ends meet without dancing. Yet she left, convinced she had to get out. Amy went forward the next Sunday night and accepted Christ as her Savior. Thankfully, the women of the church embraced her.

As the interview was winding down, I still could not figure out what it was about Amy that made her special.

With no more questions I asked her if there was anything else I needed to ask. "Ask me if I'm happy," she said coyly. I did and she gave me an enthusiastic "yes" because she no longer had to pretend. I now knew what made Amy so special. The sweet innocence lost in a lifetime of pain and sorrow had been found. She was indeed a new creation.

When I left the restaurant I was greeted by the bright sun, bursting through the dark clouds. As bright as it was, I knew there was a brighter eternal light shining in the life of the woman I left seated in the back corner of a dimly lit restaurant. And I knew her by name.

KRISTEN

Kristen and I have never met. I got her name through an organization called Citizens for Community Values (CCV) based in Memphis. Founded by Carolyn McKenzie, CCV helps deliver women from the adult entertainment industry. After Carolyn and I spoke for about 30 minutes I asked if she could put me in contact with some former dancers. She wanted to know what questions I would ask. After I read the questions to her, I heard in her voice a deep concern and love for the women she has helped find a new life. Without knowing much about me, Carolyn wanted to protect them. "Would you like to talk to one now?" she asked.

"Yes, sure," I replied.

After a few moments a quiet sweet voice said, "Hello." It was Kristen. She seemed to lack the confidence of the other dancers I had interviewed. She almost seemed timid.

Kristen has no memory of her mother. Her father was terribly abusive — physically, mentally, and sexually. Even before she was ten years old, Kristen was in and out of foster homes and was later sent to a girls' home in Mississippi. She tried to escape on several occasions to return to her father. Like so many little girls, all she wanted was her father's love. Tragically, her father perverted his love.

At ten she ran away for good, hitching a ride at a truck

stop back to Memphis. Club owners, happy to take her in, picked her up on the streets in Memphis. By 11 she was making hard-core porn movies, appearing in hard-core magazines and having sex with the club owners and anyone else the owners allowed.

"I thought I was special," said Kristen. "I was making movies and I thought that was what life was all about." The club owners bought her frilly dresses and stuffed animals, anything she wanted.

While most porn stars make a lot of money, Kristen saw very little. Her new "family" kept it all. On a night when Kristen would make $300 dancing, the owners of the club would allow her to keep $50. If she made $600–$800 on a Saturday night, she could keep $100. She never argued about the pay since she had more money than she needed because she lived with the owners. "I never had that kind of money before," said Kristen. "What I had I blew."

She spent most of her time with the owner's sister, going with her everywhere, including the club. When most girls are still playing with Barbie dolls, Kristen was caught in an abusive world of sex and drugs.

I was shocked to learn that she began dancing at the club at 14 years old. I asked Carolyn McKenzie later if Kristen looked like an adult as a young teenager. Her answer filled me with sorrow. The owners were protected by a fake ID that said Kristen was over 18 years old. Kristen danced at an early age *because* she looked like a child. The horror of child pornography left a dark imprint on my heart. This child of 14 years danced for men who lusted for children.

Not only was Kristen dancing, but she was also abusing drugs. "They kept me on drugs," she said. "I started on Valium and later did them all. I was never my own self." Drugs were everywhere in the club. They were easy to get and often provided by the owners. "They want you to get drunk and take drugs and make money for them," she said. "Once they get you hooked, they have you."

Although she had lived in the world of adult entertainment where satisfying men was her reason for existence, Kristen never got used to it. "You feel terrible after they touch you," she claimed. "I would take an alcohol bath two times a week and wash my hair with lice shampoo once a week." Kristen said she always felt dirty.

Not only did Kristen dance, but she would also escort the owner's big clients when they came into town. Her job was to fulfill their every desire. Escorting a client would bring her $300 and the owner would get $800–$1,000.

"When I refused I would get beat up," she said. "So I quit refusing." Today her body is covered with scars where she was beaten with a switch imbedded with a metal blade.

In addition to pleasing clients, Kristen would get called into an office at least weekly to have sex with an owner or the bouncer. Some women who refused the desires of the owners were killed and suicide notes left on the cars of other dancers. Kristen never refused.

At the age of 21 Kristen had seen more pain and sorrow than most people could ever imagine. "I almost came to suicide because I didn't know there was another way of life," Kristen said. She called the Salvation Army and several churches saying she wanted out, but she was told they were not prepared to help dancers. On her seventh call to a church she was told they might be able to help. They put her in touch with Carolyn McKenzie.

Carolyn brought Kristen into her home and made her feel like a part of her family. It took Kristen three months to trust Carolyn. Kristen initially thought Carolyn was an undercover cop. "I began to suffer panic attacks, scared that they would come looking for me," she said. Knowing Kristen was scared, Carolyn slept in the same room. Kristen lived with Carolyn for a year and began attending cosmetology school. She eventually moved into an apartment but still lived with Carolyn on weekends.

"Carolyn and her husband and son have been like a

family to me," she said. "They don't hurt me. I didn't know what love was all about," Kristen claimed. "I didn't think I would ever find people to love me . . . but I have."

I had trouble sleeping after my interview with Kristen. The sweet timid voice I had heard on the phone brought me to my knees pleading to God that He would restore what had been lost in the dark world of adult entertainment. As my eyes filled with tears once again, I was thankful that God knew her by name.

JULIE

I also got Julie's name from Carolyn McKenzie at CCV in Memphis. Other than her name and phone number, I knew nothing about Julie when I called. When I asked if this was a good time for us to talk on the phone, she took a moment to check on her baby in another room.

Her friendly voice and cheerful personality made conversation easy. I felt like I was talking to a good friend I hadn't seen in months. While Julie was easy to talk to, listening to her story was difficult.

Julie was on the rebound after ending an 11-year marriage when she met and married a man shortly afterwards. She thought he would help put her life back together. Little did she know that he would tear it apart.

The marriage began in Jacksonville, Florida. Julie recalled that she and her new husband made a commitment to attend church and they did for a short time. Julie soon discovered that her new husband was deeply addicted to pornography. She was dismayed and disturbed with his fascination for books, magazines, topless dancers, and phone sex. The bills for phone sex she found in his glove compartment were in the hundreds of dollars.

Saving money while married to a man trapped in pornography was extremely difficult. Her husband suggested she try topless dancing to earn the money she needed to visit her children who lived in another state. He pushed for three months before she finally gave in.

"It was the fulfillment of his sexual fantasies," said Julie. "He always wanted to see his wife dance for other men." Her first night was a disaster. She ran off the stage during the first song screaming, "I can't do this!" At the time, she didn't drink or take drugs, so onstage she knew exactly what was happening.

"It was a terrifying experience," Julie confided. Her husband consoled her by telling her that the problem was that she didn't have confidence in herself. He would "help" by getting her breast implants. He also wanted her to get her nails and hair done to give her the confidence she needed. They had to take out a loan for the implants that Julie was forced to repay.

Her husband's prodding worked in getting Julie back on the stage. "I thought as long as I did it for my husband, it was okay," said Julie. His perverted love for her brought another request, this time for group sex. Fortunately, she had the courage to turn him down flat. A short time later Julie was dancing again, yet she still lacked the confidence she needed. She learned to anesthetize her God-given modesty and decency.

"I had to get throwing-up drunk to dance again," said Julie. She also began smoking pot in the dressing room. While Julie danced at night, her husband went to other clubs and spent time with other women. After nine months, he left Julie for another woman.

Julie's husband was gone, but not her financial dependence on dancing. "I had to continue to make money to live," said Julie. "It became a necessity to make ends meet." The dancing continued and so did her abuse of drugs and alcohol. Club patrons brought her drugs in exchange for private dances. They would also wrap up drugs in dollar bills and put them in Julie's g-string.

Julie would often dance in other cities during slow months in Florida. After a hurricane destroyed her car and apartment, Julie left Jacksonville with another dancer to dance in Columbus, Georgia. While she was onstage dancing her first set, she was robbed and lost everything, including her identification. Without it, she could not dance.

One of the patrons found out about her problem and offered to help. "He was a nice man who wanted me to work modeling lingerie," she said. The promise was easy money for easy work. It turned out to be prostitution. Julie was supposed to go into a closed room and do various things for money. When a man discovered Julie was not willing to go very far, he left her after spending less than $30.

Knowing Julie was uncomfortable, her new employer wanted Julie to be his madame and run his escort service. "I couldn't look at myself in the mirror if I did that," she said. After two weeks in Columbus she returned to Florida.

During her years in dancing, Julie never stayed in one place very long. "I was always looking for someplace to be happy," she said. She danced in Florida, Alabama, Texas, Georgia, Kansas, and Tennessee. She couldn't find the happiness she longed for.

The void in her life had not been filled. Like so many other dancers, the men disgusted her. "I saw them as dollar signs," she said. "My lips would say one thing but the men never looked in my eyes." She saw men from every walk of life from blue-collar workers to U.S. senators. They were all the same and were not to be trusted.

Julie's years of emotional pain began long before her failed marriage. A minister's daughter, she grew up in a strict home in Missouri. Her father's ministry included helping struggling families. One family they were helping moved in behind Julie's house. At five, Julie was molested in the back seat of a car by a son in the family they were helping. More instances of molestation followed.

"I felt like it was my fault," said Julie. "I always wondered what I could have done." At 13 she pleaded with her father to let her go on a date to a school football game.

Her father finally gave in and Julie went to the game. Later that night her date and his brother raped her. Fearing she would get in trouble, Julie didn't tell her father.

Three years later Julie went with her father as he preached at church revival meetings. One morning in the motel Julie awoke hearing her father get out of his bed. Within moments he was in her bed. He kissed her as he rubbed himself against her. Julie flew out of bed to the bathroom. Again, Julie told no one of her dark secret. Later though, Julie told her younger sister after Julie learned that her father placed his hand on her sister's breast to "heal it." Julie confided in her sister because she was afraid what her father might do. When the family learned Julie's story, they attacked Julie, accusing her of lying.

Her current problems had a sordid history. The men she loved the most caused the pain in her past. She eventually saw that she was getting older and was going nowhere. She had dreams of being a wife and mother but couldn't find her way out of adult entertainment.

She eventually made her way to Memphis and during her first night in the club, she heard words that, strangely enough, would lead her to freedom. The words were, "Up against the wall." The club was raided.

Although charges were later dropped, Julie had no place to go. She was broke as she sat crying in a courtroom lobby. Fortunately, a woman from the special prosecutor's office got her in touch with Carolyn McKenzie.

"She talked to me and loved me," said Julie. "She helped me get out. No one had ever offered that before." Not only did Carolyn help Julie, but she also told her she would be with her even if she fell. "It was such a picture of unconditional love," said Julie. It was a love that was tested when Julie went to a country-western bar and later went home drunk with a drug dealer. She started smoking pot again and got pregnant.

At the end of herself, Julie longed to return to the

church in Missouri where she grew up. "God did something incredible in my life," said Julie. "God gave me physical healing and in my heart and emotions," she said.

During this time she was praying for the father of her unborn child to come to God. At the time he was still dealing drugs in Memphis. Over the next few months God worked in his life, too. Julie shared the gospel with him when they talked and asked him to memorize Scripture. In time, he asked Jesus into his heart.

Today Julie is still rebuilding her life in Memphis with the help of Carolyn McKenzie, the woman who offered unconditional love. Together with her husband and child, Julie is starting over. "I will never lower myself to do that again," she said. "It is only through the Lord Jesus that I have been able to rebuild my self-esteem."

After we ended our conversation, I was haunted by memories of my own past. Julie had danced in Columbus, Georgia, the city where I started using nameless topless dancers to fulfill my lust. I wanted to apologize to Julie for the women I helped keep in bondage in the same city where she had been hurt. It was too painful to say the words, because this dancer I knew by name.

I NEVER KNEW

After completing the interviews, I was filled with sadness. The words "I never knew" kept running through my mind. Like many men, I had a distorted view of women in the sex industry. I don't know how much money I pumped into the world of porn between 1976 and 1983, but today I regret every cent. I regret it because these are not the women I thought I knew. The women I paid money to see had no pain or abuse in their lives. All I saw was their monetary and sexual fulfillment and an adoration of men.

I learned about their monetary fulfillment. When these women got respectable jobs paying less, they had more money to show for their labor. The difference is that their environment changed. They no longer worked for people who used and deceived them.

I learned about their sexual fulfillment. Most women in the porn industry are trying to fill a void in their lives left vacant by their father. Not only do men keep them in bondage, but we often play a significant role in getting them started. There is no sexual fulfillment, only deception.

I learned about their adoration of men. It doesn't exist. Men never look behind the mask of sorrow that many adult entertainers wear. Without exception, every woman I spoke with said the same thing about the men they met: "I hate them." Men abused them and stripped them of their ability to trust.

What saddens me is that I see little change on the horizon. I thank God for organizations like Citizens for Community Values in Memphis and the Dallas Association for Decency. They work at the grass roots level trying to make a difference. But it's an uphill fight. Adult video stores pervade our communities. "Gentlemen's" clubs are scattered throughout our cities with packed parking lots. Adult bookstores litter landscapes across America. Local convenience stores proudly display numerous pornographic magazines on their shelves. Phone sex lines stay busy throughout the night. The Internet has become the brave new world of porn.

Hollywood has also played a role in the distortion of these women. In the movie *Strip Tease*, Demi Moore plays the role of a former FBI secretary who loses her job because of her criminal husband and loses custody of her daughter because she is now out of work. The attractive Moore turns to topless dancing. Discouraged, she vents in the dressing room surrounded by other women.

"Hey, this is honest work," one co-worker encourages. "You have nothing to be ashamed of." In a typical Hollywood statement of "truth," Moore replies, "I know that and you know that, but the judge won't."

Honest work? The world of adult entertainment is built on lies. Women deceive men by making them believe they are adored; owners deceive women by making them feel like a part of a "family"; and men deceive their wives and family by perverting their love. And God is mocked.

Mark Wahlberg, star of the 1997 film *Boogie Nights*, commented on the movie, which gave audiences a look at the porn explosion of the 1970s. "It's all about a young kid in search of love and acceptance," he says. Wahlberg claimed that adult entertainers find a support system in the sex industry where people love them no matter what.

As Satan did in the garden, pop culture mixes truth with lies. Young porn stars do look for love and acceptance, but the support system offered by the porn industry is built on a foundation of deception. The truth is that there is tremendous pain in this dark shattered world and little will change until we all know *Him* by name.

The women you read about in this chapter have performed in Dallas, Houston, Birmingham, Memphis, Los Angeles, Miami, Detroit, and Kansas City. Maybe you've never been to these cities. These women have done it all in the world of porn, from clubs to magazines and films. They have performed all kinds of sex for men who have families and jobs just like us. While you may never have seen these women, there is one thing I know for certain. Women just like Elise, Stefani, Kristen, and the others are in your hometown, and they have names, too.

5

Where in the World Is Ward Cleaver?

If you do well, will not your countenance be lifted up? And if you do not do well, sin is crouching at the door and its desire is for you, but you must master it (Gen. 4:7).

ONE OF MY FAVORITE TELEVISION SHOWS growing up was "Leave it to Beaver." It was funny and could be enjoyed by the whole family. Parents Ward and June Cleaver never raised their voices and their home was always ready for company. Their children, Wally and Theodore (known as the Beaver), were well-behaved and did well in school. Beaver was prone to mischief on occasion and Wally hung around with Eddie Haskell, who was a wise guy. I never remember seeing Ward and June's bedroom. The closest they ever came to nudity was when they would wear short-sleeve shirts.

Many years ago, long before "60 Minutes" and 'Larry King Live," Soren Kierkegard wrote, "Suppose someone invented an instrument, a convenient little talking tube which, say, could be heard over the whole land. . . . I wonder if the police would not forbid it, fearing that the whole country would become mentally deranged if it were used."[1]

My, how times have changed! Some will argue and say that the Cleaver family is not reality. That's true. But who ever said entertainment had to be reality? If television depicts reality today, then we are in big trouble.

Television may not be reality, but it is especially troublesome for men who struggle with sexual addiction. In the 1990s, sex has become one of mainstream television's hot topics.

I only have the basic cable package at home, yet I once saw a show where a woman who was being interviewed by the police in her home decided to change clothes. Right there in front of the officers she stripped down to her underwear as she answered questions about a crime.

My mind forgot the crime and focused on the creature. In Philippians 4:8, it is written, "Finally brethren, whatever is true, whatever is honorable, whatever is right, whatever is pure, whatever is lovely, whatever is of good repute, if there is any excellence and anything worthy of praise, let your mind dwell on these things." As I watched the program, nothing of good repute went through my mind. I was carried away by lust. I didn't change the channel until the scene was over. Eight months later my mind could still see her in her underwear. I allowed something into my mind that did not leave when I changed the channel.

In 1955 television broadcast hours were limited in the evening and families had only a few choices of stations. Less than a third of the American population owned a television. What in the world did everyone do for fun?

Television sets are found in 98 percent of American homes today — and toilets are found in 97 percent. While almost every home has a TV today, two-thirds of the homes have more than one set! Most Americans have cable with many channels — 24 hours a day![2]

"While I'm concerned with some of the trash that comes out of Hollywood and the so-called 25-inch sewer line into your living room, that's not my biggest concern," said Larry Poland of Mastermedia International. "My biggest concern is the consumer because the person out there that watches 'x' number of hours of television a day, even if that person calls himself a Christian . . . he does not know how to manage his family's media consumption."

Most adults today grew up on television. I can remember coming home from school, putting my books on the TV and . . . plop . . . instant couch potato! My parents never supervised what I watched. My dad hated shows like "Lost in Space" and "The Monkees" so he never watched with us. He never needed to. While most of the shows were pretty ridiculous, they didn't communicate values that were different from the ones my parents tried to teach.

Not so with shows today. In a study of 450 sixth graders that have cable at home, Oklahoma State University professor Godfrey Ellis found that an incredible 66 percent of the children watched at least one program a month that contained nudity or heavy sexual content.[3] Trust me, if sixth graders saw that much sexual content, I know the dad who struggles with temptation saw much more.

In April 1999, *Erotica USA* hit the television screen promising to be "titillating but not nasty." Fetishes and sadomasochism are just two of the disorders covered by the show. I shudder to think what the new millennium will bring into our homes via the television.

So who are these men and women who produce and direct the shows that spill into our living rooms each day? A study was done in the mid-1980s of 104 of the most influential professionals in the television industry. These professionals were described as " the cream of the television community . . . some of the most experienced and respected members of the craft." The findings concluded:

- 93 percent seldom or never attend worship services.

- 97 percent believe pregnant women have the right to decide on abortion.

- Only 5 percent strongly believe homosexuality is wrong.

- 16 percent strongly believe that adultery is wrong.[4]

Is it possible that David Frost was correct when he said, "Television is an invention that permits you to be entertained in your living room by people you would not have into your home." So it seems.

Sex has become TV's standard for programming success. A study by Lou Harris and Associates revealed the three networks broadcast 65,000 references to sexual behavior in one year.[5] In case you're calculating, that's 27 references per hour. The number will only rise in the future.

In his book *Telegarbage*, author Greg Lewis reported that "references to intercourse on television, whether verbally insinuated or contextually implied, occur between unmarried partners five times as often as married couples" and references to intercourse with prostitutes comes in second."[6]

A Florida State University study reported that a typical prime-time hour of television gave audiences 1.6 references to intercourse, 1.2 references to prostitution and rape, 4.7 sexual innuendoes, 1.8 kisses, and 1 suggestive behavior. Additionally, TV characters talk about sex or display sexual behavior 15 times an hour, or once every four minutes.

It may be interesting to know that only 9 percent of the shows that contain sexual content make any reference to the consequences of sexual acts, according to a study released by the Kaiser Family Foundation in 1999.[7]

In January 1999, *TV Guide* had a cover story entitled, "The 50 Funniest TV Moments of All Time." The 50 moments included:

- 2 involving out-of-wedlock sex
- 2 involving circumcision
- 1 involving masturbation
- 3 involving nudism

In all, 12 "funny" moments, or 20 percent, involved humor concerning subjects that are inappropriate for national television. Remember that these moments are the *funniest* of all time. Of the 12 moments that are inappropriate, only one was from a show over 20 years old. Yes, times are changing.

On the flip side, only one of those moments made it into the top ten funny TV moments.[8] Does television have to include sexual situations to be funny? Obviously not, but it seems television producers today have no desire to be funny without sex.

Is it any wonder that men struggle with sexual temptation watching TV? Men are prone to sexual fantasy and TV feeds our appetites quite well.

Ricky told me that when he is struggling with temptation, he finds himself surfing channels at night until he finds something provocative. It may be more difficult to find without cable, but it can certainly be done. There is no doubt, in our struggle with sexual temptation, television is part of the problem.

How about movies? We'll look in a later chapter at adult movies, so for now we'll concentrate on the movies you can find at your local theater and on TV. The Motion Picture Code followed from 1933 until 1966 is a far cry from what we see today. Consider the following:

- Evil, sin, crime, and wrongdoing shall not be justified."

- Indecent or undue exposure of the human body shall not be presented."

- Illicit sex relationships shall not be justified. Intimate sex scenes violating common standards of decency shall not be portrayed. Restraint and care shall be exercised in presentations dealing with sex aberrations."

Yes indeed, times have changed. Illicit sex relationships are justified today both on TV and the big screen. Hollywood's fascination with sex has become a major stumbling block for men who struggle with sexual temptation. Sadly, there is no relief in sight.

Several years ago there was an action movie with a well-known actor and a beautiful actress. In one particular scene, the woman stripped for the man. This was *not* an "R" rated movie, yet the scene in question sent my mind to places where it should not go. I knew instantly that I was not alone in my fascination. I knew other men across the country felt as I did.

Have you noticed an increase in "R" rated movies? In 1975, about 5 percent of the movies were rated "R." Today the figure is over 65 percent. Each "R" rated movie averages over 50 acts of violence, sex, and profanity. Walter Scott, columnist for *Parade* magazine, said that screenwriters seek the "R" rating to attract teenagers "who shun PG and PG-13 films, seeing them as a sign of immaturity."

Hollywood is out of control. Their fascination with sex and perversion has played a key role in the loss of our moral bearings today. They continue to draw the line in the sand closer and closer to the water and we're drowning.

"There should be more sex in movies," said Don Simpson, producer of *Flashdance* and *An Officer and a Gentleman*. "It's about time that kids who are 13 years old are shown making love."[9] Is that the belief of mainstream America? Hardly, but it is the belief of someone who makes movies for our families to "enjoy."

It's obvious that Hollywood is not interested in returning to the days when 5 percent of the movies were rated "R." They are on a course to put "G" rated movies out of business. How can we stop the trend? Stop seeing "R" rated movies. Every time you go, you are voting "yes" to more "R" rated movies. Remember, with the rating comes the nudity or acts of sex. An "R" rated movie has the potential to send a man on a search and destroy mission.

No "R" rated movies? A bit drastic maybe. Replace the movies with something wholesome. Need ideas? How about writing an encouraging note to your pastor. Send a letter to a missionary. Take your family out and take pictures. Look at old photos as a family. Go feed the ducks. Do a jigsaw puzzle. Have a family concert using glasses filled with water. Dale and Karen Mason wrote a wonderful book called *How to Get the Best Out of TV* filled with many more entertaining suggestions for married and single men alike. I highly recommend its reading.

Guys, I just have trouble with the logic that TV and movies are nothing more than enjoyable entertainment. Somehow, I can't picture myself sitting next to Jesus with His approval as Demi Moore or Sharon Stone undress. I believe it grieves Him.

There is nothing harmless about TV and movies today, particularly for the man struggling with sexual temptation. We need to be on the alert, careful what we put in our minds.

Ward Cleaver in the 1950s and Al Bundy in the 1990s. Think about how our culture has changed and where we will be as a nation when our great-grandchildren are watching TV. It just might keep you up at night.

1 Charles Colson, *Against the Night* (Ann Arbor, MI: Vine Books, 1989), p. 41.
2 Dale and Karen Mason, *How to Get the Best Out of TV* (Nashville, TN: Broadman & Holman Publishers, 1996), p. 14.
3 Ibid., p. 39.
4 Ibid., p. 27.

5 Ibid., p. 31.

6 Ibid., p. 31, quoting Gregg A. Lewis, *Telegarbage* (Nashville, TN: Thomas Nelson Publishers, 1977).

7 Ed Bark, "TV Indicates Few Risks in Sex, Study Says," *Dallas Morning News*, February 10, 1999.

8 Katalin Korossy editorial, Maryland Coalition Against Pornography, Inc., February 1999.

9 "Lincoln Wasn't Pro-Choice," *Conservative Digest*, February 1985, p. 35.

6

Satan's Dynamic Duo: Hugh and Larry

For all that is in the world, the lust of the flesh
and the lust of the eyes and the boastful pride of
life, is not from the Father, but is from the world
(1 John 2:16).

MAGAZINES. FOR MOST MEN, THIS is where addiction begins.
In my survey of over 100 Christian men, 95 percent said
their first exposure to pornography was through magazines.
When I asked them where the pornographic magazines
came from, here's what the men said:

First exposure	Percentage
Friend's house	77%
Father's pornography	13%
Self-purchased	1%
Other – (found it)	9%

Magazines are fairly easy to find; kids certainly don't have trouble getting their hands on them. Only 1 percent of my respondents bought a magazine on his own. For the other 99 percent, someone else made the purchase. That fact — that 77 percent of the men had their first exposure at a friend's house — should serve as a reminder that we need to know with whom our sons hang around. Sadly, for 13 percent of the respondents, it was their own father.

A few years ago, you might find *Playboy, Penthouse,* and *Hustler* on the shelves of most convenience stores. Today some convenience stores carry over 50 different titles. Plastic wrappers hide the magazine covers, but if you take a good look you can see the face of a young woman. More than likely, she has an inviting smile. Pornographers want you to see her. Get an eyeful and let Satan do the rest.

Some men try to protect themselves when they purchase pornography by making up their own "rules" about buying magazines in a store. When "Bryan" gave in to the temptation to buy pornographic magazines, it had to be a man behind the counter and no one else could be in the store. Sometimes he would wait in his car until the store had no customers and the coast was clear. As a leader in his church, "Bryan" was consumed in shame. There are many other men like "Bryan" who have similar rules for buying pornography. The thought of getting caught is unthinkable, so Christian men will go to great measures to keep their sin a secret.

Some convenience stores do not carry pornographic magazines. Those are the stores where we need to shop. Decency groups throughout the country are waging a war on this front to rid communities of pornography in convenience stores. It's a tough fight.

Of course, many men see magazines when the U.S. Postal Service delivers them straight to their homes. To avoid the embarrassment of buying them in a convenience store, we can subscribe! We'll even get an occasional invitation. *Playboy* publisher Richard Kinsler sent a letter to the magazine's "preferred customers." He wrote:

> In appreciation of being one of our most valued customers, we're sending you this unique package of special offers designed to help you get the *most out of life*. Exclusively brought together for you by *PLAYBOY*.
>
> Please take a moment to look inside to see which of these exclusive offers grab your interest. As a *PLAYBOY* customer, I'm sure you'll find something here that will fit your *passion for living*." (italics mine)

Oh, my . . . it sounds like he is doing us a big favor. He wants to help men to "get the most out of life" that fits their "passion for living."

Magazines cover all aspects of pornography imaginable. Some magazines, like *Playboy,* are owned by wealthy corporations and others are very small operations. "I didn't have a lot of money," said Lily Braindrop, founding editor of a low-budget magazine. "I started the magazine with about $100. I have stuff that is really gory or really violent or sadomasochistic or really gender-bent because I think that's the job or the role of fantasy in the human experience — to give you permission to do all these things."[1] From Braindrop's statement it's obvious that character and decency are not common attributes for magazine editors.

Pornographers know how to get a man's attention. Next to the nude body of a voluptuous young woman in a pornographic magazine advertisement are the following words, "If women have been a mystery to you, let *Chic* magazine unveil their mysteries. *Chic's* ladies have nothing to hide. . . . They know all and show all! . . . You'll know all!" Sound educational? I don't think so. Pornographers don't want to educate potential readers. They want to entice men to look further and to ensnare them with the lie that they will offer freedom, wisdom, and power. The truth is that they will deliver bondage.

If you ask men to name a pornographic magazine, I suspect the first one that comes to mind is *Playboy*. The founder's name is almost a household name. His friends know him simply as "Hef."

Hugh Hefner was born in 1926 in Chicago. His father was a descendant of William Bradford, the puritan governor of Massachusetts. Both of Hefner's parents were raised as staunch Methodists. He grew up during the depression and rarely saw his father.

"The only time we really saw him was on holidays or Sundays," said Hefner. His father was gone when he woke up and back after he was in bed. Hefner learned to rely on friends who "supplied the emotional connections that I did not find in the home," said Hefner.

Hefner developed a creative talent that he often expressed with cartoons. He fell in love with Millie Williams and followed her to the University of Illinois. While at the university he became the editor of the campus humor magazine, *Shaft*. Under his leadership, *Shaft* profiled the university's prettiest and most-promising women in a feature called co-ed of the month.[2]

During the time Hefner was at the University of Illinois, Indiana University professor Alfred Kinsey published his study on human sexuality. Kinsey's findings reported that 86 percent of American men experienced sexual intercourse before marriage, 70 percent had sex with prostitutes, and 40 percent engaged in extramarital intercourse.[3] Little attention was paid to the fact that Kinsey's sample was weighted disproportionately by homosexuals, prisoners, and other social deviants. Hefner, like many of his post-World War II generation, bought Kinsey's teachings hook, line, and sinker.

The study "confirmed . . . that our attitudes toward sex

were not only very repressive; they were hurtful and hypo-
critical," claimed Hefner. Kinsey provided seeds that took
root in the life of the future pornographer.

Not all was well on the personal front, however. Millie
left the university and took a job as a schoolteacher. Hefner
stayed in Illinois to complete his last semester. While they
were apart, Millie slept with another man. Hefner called it
the "single most devastating experience of my life."

In spite of their difficulties, Hef and Millie married in
1949. Hefner struggled in a few jobs before he decided to
start *Stag Party*, a men's magazine which would include
photographs of nude women. Since he had the rights to a
nude photo of Marilyn Monroe taken before she became a
star, he felt he had a sure-fire hit. "I had less to lose," boasted
Hefner. No other magazine was willing to take the risk of
sending obscenity through the mail. *Stag Party* later became
Playboy when he had to change the title after complaints
from an outdoor adventure magazine called *Stag*.

In November 1953 the first issue of *Playboy* hit the
newsstands with Marilyn Monroe on the cover. As pre-
dicted, the magazine was a tremendous success and Hefner
committed himself to work. Leaving his wife and daughter
alone, Hefner even slept at the office.

As his exposure to pornography increased, so did his
sexual appetite. "I'd step out of a meeting and go and make
love with somebody in the middle of the afternoon and go
back to the meeting," boasted Hefner.

When news of Hefner's adultery reached Millie, she
was obviously hurt. "I was very crushed," she said. "In a way
it was cruel what he did." Hefner discovered what many
other men and women have learned. Lust has consequences.
Hef and Millie divorced in 1959.

"When I started the magazine I didn't figure that would
be a passport to the end of the marriage," admitted Hefner.
"I didn't think on those terms at all, but that's what it turned
out to be." Even though pornography had destroyed his

marriage, Hefner never heard the wake-up call.

In 1960 Hefner opened his first Playboy Club, complete with the famous Playboy bunnies. Comedian Dick Gregory called it "Disneyland for adults." The club had a huge following the minute it opened the doors.

Since his first issue in 1953, Hefner stayed on the cutting edge of pornography. Some of his bunnies and centerfolds have become famous. More have been destroyed. Life at the Playboy mansion was reported to be luxurious, sensuous, and satisfying.

"*Playboy* has always been supportive of me and they've become like a family to me," said one Playmate.[4] Her false view of family deceived many of the mansion's tenants and guests.

Another Playmate said, "I experienced everything from date rape to physical abuse to group sex. . . . The group sex held in Hefner's mansion was accompanied by the pornographic movie *The Devil in Miss Jones*.[5]

Celebrating the magazine's 35th anniversary in 1989, *Playboy's* January issue reported, "*Playboy* freed a generation from guilt about sex, changed some laws and helped launch a revolution or two. . . . So you may not think it immodest of us to say *Playboy* is the magazine that changed America."[6]

The change Hefner refers to is hardly worth boasting about. America is dying in the wake of our moral vacuum. Now in his seventies, Hefner said, "The single driving force in my life is looking for that perfect world where the words to the songs are true, where you are given unquestioning, non-judgmental, total love. I've spent my life looking for that world. And it's been a wonderful adventure."[7]

Hefner has spent his life searching for a love which is found only in God. The adventure he boasts of on earth will lead to an eternity of separation from love.

While Hefner was the first big name in pornographic magazines, Larry Flynt is the most outrageous. The founder of *Hustler* magazine was born in poverty in eastern Kentucky in 1942. His father returned home from World War II a stranger and turned to moonshine to drown his frustrations.

In addition to problems with his father, Flynt's mother was a topic of local gossip. She is alleged to have committed adultery. "We had no family life," said Larry's brother Jimmy. "I'm sure that had an effect on us both."

After the death of Larry's 4-year-old sister, his parents divorced. Larry ran away and was molested by a man who offered him a ride. As an adult he joined the military but was discharged for low-test scores. He returned home to the moonshine business. When his father was late in paying for a delivery of illegal liquor, Larry bashed his father's head with a jug of whiskey.

Flynt tried the Armed Forces again, this time the Navy. He was able to stay in the service but spent most of his salary on prostitutes. One night he claimed he spent the night with 20 women.[8]

In January 1964, Flynt received the following medical report at the U.S. Naval Hospital in Portsmouth, Virginia. "This 23-year-old Radarman Second Class has had reoccurring difficulties for one year. His symptoms have at various times included lightheadedness, spells of pain and numbness of neck and arms and face, insomnia, arrested breathing while asleep, hyperventilation, hysteria (whole body shaking) etc. He has had a great deal of psychic trauma centered around his sex and marital life. But even with insight and extensive support and superficial psychotherapy by several medical officers, he has been unable to cope. Diagnosed with 'anxiety reaction.' " Flynt received an administrative discharge seven months later.[9]

At 23, twice divorced and out of the Navy, he decided to try his hand at the lounge business, opening the Hustler Club.

His appetite for women continued. "One lady was

never enough for him," said Jimmy Flynt. "He had to have six, eight, ten women in one day."[10] By 1971 he was the father of four children by four different women. His sex addiction was out of control. "Dad would later say that he didn't mind a man having sex with his wife, daughter, or grandmother, provided the man asked his permission first," said his daughter, Tonya Flynt-Vega.[11]

In July 1974, he published the first issue of *Hustler* magazine. It was a flop. However, Larry didn't quit. *Hustler*'s readership began to grow by featuring articles and photographs which no other men's magazine had ever had the indecency to show before.

In 1977 Larry met President Carter's sister, Ruth Carter Stapleton. When Larry claimed to have seen the apostle Paul on the *Hustler* jet in November of that year, he fell to his knees and Stapleton, who was on the jet with him, baptized him. However, he never left the porn business. "Today instead of hustling for sex," said Larry, "we're going to be hustling for the Lord."

The changes he made to his pornographic magazine upset his staff. His girlfriend Althea was certainly not happy. "God may have walked into your life," she said. "But twenty million (dollars) a year just walked out."[12] In 1978 Larry was shot by a racist gunman named Joseph Paul Franklin. Franklin shot Flynt after he published a photo spread called, "Georgia Sweet Peach and Butch."[13] The sexually involved spread depicted a white woman with a black man. Flynt's injury resulted in chronic, extreme pain. The pain apparently edged God out of his life.

Althea became addicted to heroin and contracted AIDS. In 1987 she drowned in a bathtub with Larry in the next room.[14]

In 1997, Hollywood portrayed Flynt as a First Amendment patriot in the movie *The People vs. Larry Flynt*. Larry's daughter, Tonya Flynt-Vega, was upset about the film's distortion of his life. She claimed that her father had molested her as a child. Before she was ten, he showed her *Hustler* cartoons of "Chester the Molester." Saying he would never publish lies, Larry got his young naked daughter into bed and had sex with her.

"He asked me to touch him," said Tonya. "I was shaking, wanting to cry, to vomit, to run from the room. 'No, Tonya,' I told myself. 'You don't know what a father's love is supposed to be. That's why he was showing you his magazine. That's why he said he couldn't lie in the magazine, couldn't have something wrong. This must truly be what a father does with his daughter when he loves her.' "[15]

"I wouldn't wish my childhood on anybody because it was so painful," Tonya said. "I suffered so much abuse by my father, every kind of abuse."[16] Larry called her a habitual liar with mental problems.

Hugh and Larry . . . the dynamic duo of porn magazines. Neither had a decent relationship with his father. No one was there to show them what it means to be a man. Both committed their lives to the business of destroying women and men alike. Both had several wake-up calls that fell on deaf ears. They have made bad choices and one day they will be held accountable.

The heyday for pornographic magazines was in the 1970s. With video, cable, and the Internet, magazine sales have dropped significantly. For many young boys, however, magazines continue to be the springboard into pornography. If that isn't bad enough, pornographic magazines play a role in the corruption of our culture.

Consider the following statistics from the American Family Association:

(1) states with the highest readership of men's magazines have the highest incidence of reported rape.

(2) 85 percent of the revenue from pornographic magazines finds its way into the pockets of organized crime.

And pornographic magazines destroy marriages. Noting the appeal of *Playboy's* centerfold, Gay Talese wrote, "She was their mental mistress. She stimulated them in solitude, and they often saw her picture while making love to their wives. She was an almost special species who exists within the eye and mind of the observer and she offered everything imaginable. She was always available at bedside, was totally controllable . . . she behaved in a way that real women did not, which was the essence of fantasy."[17] No wife can compete with the deception of a centerfold's perfect sexuality.

In 1977 *Penthouse* sold 4.6 million copies. In 1996, the number was just over a million.[18] For magazines to survive in the next millennium alongside videos and the Internet, they have to change. *Penthouse* took a leap "forward" by showing people actually engaged in sexual intercourse in its July 1997 issue. Such photos are normally considered taboo by soft-core peddlers; publisher Bob Guccione said he thought, "the time was right." He added, "We are breaking new ground in how forthright a magazine can be. We are showing art, love, and creative expression." More than likely it is an act of desperation.

Hugh and Larry. Eternity will be a long time for them to reflect on how they have changed America. Satan has used them well.

1 Sylvia Plachy and James Ridgeway, *Red Light — Inside the Sex Industry* (New York: Powerhouse Books, 1996), p. 71.
2 Hugh Hefner biography video, A & E Television Network, 1996.
3 Judith A. Reisman, *Soft Porn Plays Hardball — Its Tragic Effects on Women, Children and the Family* (Lafayette, LA: Huntington House Publishers, 1991), p. 36.
4 Hugh Hefner biography video, A & E Television Network.
5 James Lambert, *Porn in America* (Lafayette, LA: Huntington House Publishers, 1997), p. 34.
6 Reisman, *Soft Porn Plays Hardball,* p. 10.
7 Hugh Hefner biography video, A & E Television Network.

8 Larry Flynt biography video, A & E Television Network.

9 Tonya Flynt-Vega, *My Journey from Fear to Faith* (Louisville, KY: Westminster/John Knox Press, 1998), p. 36.

10 Larry Flynt biography video, A & E Television Network.

11 Flynt-Vega, *My Journey from Fear to Faith*, p. 48.

12 Larry Flynt biography video, A & E Television Network.

13 Flynt-Vega, *My Journey from Fear to Faith*, p. 142.

14 Larry Flynt biography video, A & E Television Network.

15 Flynt-Vega, *My Journey from Fear to Faith*, p. 48.

16 Larry Flynt biography video, A & E Television Network.

17 Susan Griffin, *Pornography and Silence* (New York: Harper & Row Publishers, 1981), p. 34.

18 *American Family Association Journal*, American Family Association, August 1997, p. 9.

7

VCR —— Very Corrupt Rendezvous

> For by these He has granted to us His precious and magnificent promises, in order that by them you might become partakers of the divine nature, having escaped the corruption that is in the world by lust (2 Pet. 1:4).

MY WIFE, KATHY, HELPED ME with the title of this chapter. I came up with VC, but I couldn't figure out the R. I handed her the dictionary and before she opened it, she said, "How about rendezvous?"

Wow! She hit it right on the head. Adult movies really are a rendezvous for lust between a man and women he doesn't even know. For married men, their wives are probably asleep upstairs. These movies are big business doing big damage to families.

While some married couples watch adult movies together, most Christian men who watch them do it alone.

"Scott" told me that in his home growing up, his father once played the porn video *The Devil in Mrs. Jones* for the family. Thirteen-year-old "Scott" was fascinated by the video. "Scott" didn't get a chance to finish the video, but his appetite was aroused. He saw plenty in later years to make up for it.

Make no mistake about it — adult videos are big business. In the 1970s men had to go to seedy theaters to see X-rated titles. The risk was often too great for the Christian man struggling with sexual temptation. Things have changed today with technology. Most people have videocassette recorders and several video stores within a few minutes from their home.

Chain video stores like Blockbuster normally don't carry X-rated titles, but many of the R-rated movies can be instruments to feed lust, too. The phrase "sex sells" certainly applies to movies.

To a man struggling with sexual temptation, the XXX-rated videos are devastating. These videos are found at adult bookstores and local video stores. The Mom and Pop video stores have many family movies and plenty of current titles. Often they have a back room not much bigger than a large closet. The door is clearly marked for adults only.

I went into one store late at night and browsed through the family titles until there was no one else in the store. I walked up to the woman working behind the counter and asked her if she knew what the videos in the back room were doing to families. With my question I handed her a tract. She gazed at the cover of the tract and her eyes welled up with tears.

"Yes I know," she said. "My marriage was destroyed because of my husband's addiction to adult videos." She explained that she had talked to the manager about getting rid of the movies but he wanted to expand the room since one-third of his business came from that large closet filled with adult videos. Her comment shouldn't come as much of a surprise since 52 percent of males ages 18-34 find it desirable for video stores to carry adult products.[1] We talked for a few moments and I encouraged her to take a stand. I sent both her and the owner a letter the following week. When I went back a few weeks later, I discovered that she no longer worked there. The room, however, was as busy as ever.

Her comment about sales volume was on target with video stores across the nation. According to *Adult Video News*, many video stores reap great profits from sexually oriented titles. Adult titles in a video store in Maryland make up 25 percent of their inventory and 50 percent of the sales and rentals. Adult Video News listed video stores in New York, California, Illinois, Michigan, Virginia, and other states that reported similar results.[2]

Not only are porn videos accessible near our homes, but for the men who travel, they are as easy as turning on the television in hotels. "It does generate a little income," said Gordon Lambourne, a spokesman for Marriott. "We offer it because there's a demand for it, and because our competition offers it, too."[3] How tragic that hotels feel that in order to get customers, they have to provide pornographic movies.

Hotels go to incredible measures to take care of travelers while they are away from their families. Clean sheets, new soap, and shampoo on a daily basis, chains for the door, and sometimes even mints on the pillow. All to make us comfortable. I don't get that kind of treatment at home! On the road I feel pampered. Unfortunately, hotels often provide pornographic movies. What happened to taking care of travelers? Each time a traveler walks into the room, he has to make a decision to not turn to the adult channels.

For the man who has been away from his family for several days and had a tough week on the road, the temptation can be overpowering. Several regular travelers have told me that Thursday night is the worst. If they are going to watch a porn movie, Thursday night is their last chance before returning home Friday. Their last chance comes when they are the most tired, emotionally and physically.

To make matters worse, the hotels make sure you know that your movie choices are to remain confidential. Before the pornographic movie begins, a message on the screen states that movies are not billed by the title of the film. Hotels looking out for our "best interests" protect our shame, but they endanger marriages and families for the almighty dollar. Remember that the next time you find a hotel to stay in.

On an encouraging note, Omni Hotel owner Bob Rowling made a $4 million decision to get rid of adult movies and magazines from his hotels. "Money is not the issue in this matter," said Peter Strebel, Omni vice-president of marketing. "Not all business decisions should be fiscally driven. We believe that it is the right thing to do for Omni hotels, our associates, and customers." Next time you travel, find an Omni Hotel to stay in. They care about your family.

How can wives today compete with the "sex-starved women" who make pornographic movies? Video porn stars have a sexual appetite that is never satisfied . . . or so we are led to believe.

Men, the battle is becoming more intense. Today, adult entertainment is a $9 billion industry. And it's growing. Where in the world are these videos coming from? Would you believe that the world's largest producer is the United States, centered in California's San Fernando Valley?[4] The San Fernando Valley has become the Ellis Island of adult entertainment for many men and women who dream of acting careers. The region's favorable climate and large influx of females looking for acting jobs makes the region attractive, according to Los Angeles police detective Robert Navarro.[5]

Over the past five years, pornographic video rentals have increased 100 percent. Not surprisingly, adult videos account for 25 percent of video revenue.[6] According to the

Los Angeles Daily News, an estimated 1,500 adult titles hit the market in 1986. That number dropped in the late eighties, but in 1992 the number of adult videos began to skyrocket. In 1997, 7,970 new titles hit the market. Compare that number to the 231 feature films released by Hollywood that same year.[7] The porn industry averages more titles in two weeks than Hollywood releases in a year![8]

The economics of porn movies is staggering. *Deep Throat*, the huge hit of the seventies, generated revenue of over $50 million but cost just $25,000 to make. That's quite a profit. It remains a booming business. In 1989, adult film and video grossed $992 million. That figure rose to $1.6 billion by 1992 and just five years later, in 1997, the number was up to $4.2 billion.[9]

"We want to go to mainstream America," said porno king Steve Hirsch. "We want the guy who likes a good sexy movie on HBO to see that we make good quality movies." Hirsch is the president of Vivid Videos, where contract girls make $1,000-$1,500 a day. Contract girls may shoot six to eight films a year for a total of 20 shooting days. The rest of their money comes from headlining at local strip clubs where they may earn $5,000 to $20,000 a week. That's right — a week. I've wondered how many of those dollars came from Christian men.

Pornographers like Steve Hirsch are not creators of dreams, they are destroyers of dreams. Where did Hirsch get his start? His father was a pornographer. Even his sister heads up production at Vivid Videos. The Hirsch family is a staunch supporter of First Amendment freedom. "What I don't like is when people say I don't have the right to do this," said Steve. "People have the right to choose what they view in their own homes."

Some of the women see adult movies as an avenue to making movies in Hollywood. Fat chance. Porn stars have careers that normally last less than three years. To retired porn stars, acting doors are locked and shut with the keys thrown away. Their dreams are gone along with their self-esteem.

One of Vivid Video's biggest contract girls is a woman named Janine. Janine got her big "break" after posing in *Penthouse* in 1987 at the age of 18. In 1992, she made the jump to adult movies. Strangely enough, Janine would only act opposite women "out of respect for my husband." She has had more "luck" than most contract girls with a career lasting more than five years. She is not however, without her fears. "I think about getting a normal job, going to school, but people would say, 'Aren't you . . . ?' Every day, I want to be a school teacher," said Janine, "but I can just imagine the parents saying that I can't be around their kids."

Another adult star, Jill Kelly, sees little escape from this business. "I chose a different path, and it's too late to change now," she said. "It's forever. The commitment of a lifetime."[10] It seems that adult movies do more than just destroy families.

Kelly's family was destroyed, too, as a result of her acting in pornographic films. Her husband, Cal Jammer, was involved in an adulterous relationship off the set, which upset her greatly. When Cal got angry at her response, she left home, leaving Cal devastated. (Don't bother trying to make sense of that.)

"He wanted to have a normal job," Jill said. "And he wanted me to stay home and have kids and go to church on Sundays." Cal realized this would never happen so one night he stood outside her house with a gun to his head. "This is for you, babe," he said, and pulled the trigger.[11] Surrounded by tragedy, Jill Kelly's "commitment of a lifetime" seems more like a death sentence.

Who can forget the name of Linda Lovelace? She was the star of the famed pornographic movie *Deep Throat*. Lovelace was beaten and imprisoned by a man named Chuck Traynor, who forced her to act in pornographic films. Traynor later became her husband. During her relationship with Traynor, Lovelace was forced to have sex with other men both as a prostitute and as a favor he extended to his friends. The list goes on with other obscenities too inappropriate to describe here.

Lovelace was beaten whenever she cried or showed tears. Like many other women in pornography, she learned to place a fake smile on her face. Real feelings were replaced with a mask. Her audience never cared to see behind her mask.

"They wouldn't have cared if I was an inflatable plastic doll, a puppet," Lovelace said. That's the way lust works. All we care about is ourselves. For Lovelace, her heartache led to drugs, which helped her do things she hated. Once during a shooting she was instructed to urinate on another actress. When she had difficulty doing it, she was told that if she didn't do it, she would play the role of the other actress.[12] Lovelace's life was in shambles.

"I want to set the record straight," said Lovelace. "I was not a willing participant. I was a victim of *Deep Throat*. Every time someone views that movie, they're viewing me being raped."[13]

Sadly, Lovelace's story is not unique. "There are plenty of Chuck Traynors out there," said Lovelace. "And an endless supply of young girls who are young, trusting, gullible, and sometimes a little stupid. And it is certain that these people will, from time to time, come together. By the time they are pried apart, incredible damage can be done."[14]

Colleen Applegate was one young woman with high hopes for a film career. Her father, Phil, said in a *People* magazine interview, "I think 18-year-old kids with stars in their eyes, if you flash enough money at them, there isn't too much they're not going to do, or justify in their own mind that it's really not wrong."

Applegate starred in over 30 films. She ended her life at the age of 20 in an apparent suicide. "The pornographers used her well," said her mother Karen. "They're still using her."[15]

While some of the women look to porn videos in hope of an acting job, others are runaway youths. Lisa Maria Abato, involved in adult entertainment for three years, in a public statement to the Los Angeles City Council said the "sex industry's lure to many runaway youths is overwhelming."[16]

For many "actresses," all they have to show for their time in the business are drug and alcohol addictions, destroyed families, and shattered self-esteem. That's quite a price to pay to fulfill the lust of men who never cared enough to look behind the mask.

There is another price these women pay. In an industry where sex is the order of the day, disease leaves its mark. The adult video community now encourages the use of condoms because so many performers have tested HIV positive or have contracted AIDS.

"It's a fairly big step," said Paul Fishbein, publisher of *Adult Video News*. "It's interesting that it takes people to get a little bit scared for them to be proactive."[17] Interesting? I thought it was sad.

"We have made a decision to go 100 percent condoms in all our movies," said Vivid president Steve Hirsch. "We believe that this is a positive step in protecting the health of the industry and the personnel that are so vital to its existence."[18] Don't be fooled. Hirsch cares only about profits and nothing about the women trapped in this horrible industry.

Evil Angel owner John Stagliano is a bit more honest. "It never has been and would not be my position to regulate how people engage in sex in the videos I sell; only that they make hot videos that are salable, up to a certain standard. How they do it is their own business."[19]

One adult actress, Tricia Devereaux, was shocked when she tested HIV positive. "I'm really hoping," said Devereaux, ". . . that somehow some freak thing happened in my private life, whether it was at the dentist's office, or God knows where this could have happened."[20] Oh, God certainly knows how this happened and I think Devereaux does, too.

For the Christian man, the sin of pornography and adult entertainment is always unsettling. There is never a peace in the midst of sin for the man who loves Jesus. In 1 John 3:9, it is written, "No one who is born of God practices sin, because His seed abides in him; and he cannot sin, because he is born of God." If a man who claims to be a Christian sins without shame and guilt, then he needs to re-examine his profession of faith.

Adult movies are not just a problem for men in trench coats in a seedy part of town. Christian men struggle, too. "During my video seduction," said one pastor, "I experienced a perplexing spiritual struggle. I rationalized viewing discrete sex and partial nudity. I thought I was mature enough to handle this. There's nothing wrong with merely viewing these things. I'm not the one doing them. Yet deep within my heart, I knew I was guilty."

The pastor knew firsthand about the absence of peace in the midst of sinning. "On a Saturday night I went to a video shop, intending to get a family movie. But I found myself laying $3 on the counter for an X-rated movie. 'It's just curiosity, not lust,' I told myself. 'Perhaps as a Christian leader I should be aware of what the world is consuming.' What I saw was ugly. The film degraded men and women. The beauty of human sexuality as God designed it and as I had experienced it in marriage was absent. I felt empty, cheated, and defeated."[21]

Many Christian men could tell a similar tale of feeling "empty, cheated, and defeated." The good news is that there is a path to victory. Hang on for the ride, we're almost there.

1 "VSDA Survey Shows Importance of Adult Product," *Adult Video News*, April 1998, p. 64.
2 "Retailer Reports — Statistically Strong," *Adult Video News*, December 1998, p. 16.

3 "Adult Industry Spins a Web of Profit," *Fort Lauderdale Sun-Sentinel*, November 13, 1997.

4 Lynn Snowden, "Deep Inside the Valley of Sin," *George*, March 1998, p. 116.

5 James Lambert, *Porn in America* (Lafayette, LA: Huntington House Publishers, 1997), p. 62.

6 Snowden, "Deep Inside the Valley of Sin," p. 116.

7 "An Uneasy Peace? Valley's Porn Industry Thrives — Quietly," *Los Angeles Daily News*, March 29, 1998.

8 Snowden, "Deep Inside the Valley of Sin," p. 116.

9 "Porn Pays," *Los Angeles Daily News*, November 20, 1997.

10 Snowden, "Deep Inside the Valley of Sin," p. 116–118, 140.

11 Frederica Mathews-Green, "Overthrown by Eros," *World Magazine*, November 18, 1995.

12 Susan Griffin, *Pornography and Silence* (New York: Harper & Row Publishers, 1981), p. 112–114.

13 "Burned-out Porn Stars," *Fox Files*, March 25, 1999.

14 Linda Lovelace, *Ordeal* (Secaucus, NJ: Citadel Press, 1980), p. 251.

15 Lambert, *Porn in America*, p. 66.

16 Ibid.

17 "Porno Condoms," AP Wire, May 1, 1998.

18 "Top XXX Producers Decide to Go Condom Only," *Adult Video News*, June 1998.

19 Ibid.

20 "Porno Condoms."

21 "Video Seduction," *Moody Magazine*, March 1995.

8

Sorry, Wrong Number

Let no unwholesome word proceed from your mouth, but only such a word as is good for edification according to the need of the moment, that it may give grace to those who hear (Eph. 4:29).

I WAS WATCHING AN OLD MOVIE at home late one Friday night. The movie was corny but I wasn't very tired so it held my interest. At a commercial break there was a beautiful, scantily clad woman that wanted the viewer to call her for adult conversation. "Pick up the phone," she pleaded with a seductive smile as the 800 number flashed across the screen. She didn't want adult conversation. She was looking for phone sex with a man who would later get stuck with the bill at $3.99 a minute. Could you have imagined such a commercial 30 years ago? Two wonderful communications tools of the 20th century, television and the telephone, are being used by pornographers to trap men into the expensive world of phone sex. And it's working quite well.

What exactly is phone sex? Quite simply, it's talking

dirty over the phone to someone who talks dirty back. The sole purpose is for the man to have an orgasm as he listens to the erotic talk of a stranger.

Men can find the phone numbers while watching late night television, or they can find them in abundance in the back of pornographic magazines. Several years ago all the phone sex calls were made to 800 and 900 numbers. When I asked a group of men about the advantage of 800 numbers, the answer was simple. "It's free," they said. Well, that's the first lie. When you call an 800 number you'll often hear a recorded seductive female voice inviting you to call her at a 900 number. So much for the "free" call. And many of the 900 lines are no more than recorded messages. The recording explains, "900 block? No problem." Now you get the chance to provide your credit card number. That's right — credit card. I have trouble understanding why anyone would give his credit card number to a phone sex operator, but it happens . . . a lot.

"It made me a little nervous at first," said Mark, "but I figured I could dispute the charges as a bogus claim with the credit card company." Several times Mark had to call his credit card company disputing a claim.

If you don't want to use a credit card, there are other options. You can call an oversees 011 number which the seductive recorded voice provides. Need more options? How about this . . . hit the number one on your phone and they'll call you right back — collect, of course! My, that's easy.

"With overseas calls made to 011 numbers," said Mark, "you can plan on staying on the line for 10–15 minutes before you talk to anyone. And with the overseas numbers, you can't always understand them nor can they understand you."

Men are stimulated not only by what they see, but also by what they hear. There is a sense of control, protection, and harmlessness since men don't have to come in contact with the woman. Actually, the unknown woman divulging sexual fantasies in explicit language over a telephone line has men trapped by their own lust and the trap comes with a hefty price tag.

Since its inception in the late 1980s, the phone sex industry quickly became a billion-dollar business, generating $2.4 billion in revenues in the early years.[1] According to *Time Magazine*, Pacific Bell earned $13.5 million in revenues in its first 12 months of contracting phone sex exchanges local to the New York City area.[2] A 1995 *New York Newsday* article reported that the FCC records indicated that calls from the United States to the island Republic of Sao Tome increased "from 4,300 in 1991 to 360,000 in 1993. Sao Tome? Where in the world is that? With over 4,000 international phone sex lines throughout the United States, Americans are dialing up 15 million minutes a month.[3] Per-minute billing requires the customer to keep track of how long he has been on the phone. Estimates are usually short of actual charges.

The goal of phone sex operators is simple. They want to take you from being a first-time caller to a regular customer. Phone sex is easy because you don't have to confront anyone face to face. Men masturbate during the call that normally lasts between three and seven minutes. When orgasm is achieved, men often hang up without saying goodbye. Pretty simple. Time on the phone just cost $2.99 to $5.99 a minute.

Hours may be spent on a phone sex line over several weeks before a caller receives his first bill. Customers may be astounded by their phone sex charges, but the prospect of erotic fantasy lures them back again and again.

The operator's desire is to keep a customer on the phone as long as possible and they'll say whatever it takes. Some companies have pre-recorded messages instructing the caller to "press 1 for a blonde, 2 for a brunette."[4] Many phone sex companies have choices that are much more deviant, including domination, bestiality, rape, and torture. And yes, some operators will even pretend to be children.[5]

Operators try to develop relationships with callers, sometimes leading them to believe that they will meet someday. To build a relationship, the operator might say, "You're by far the best man I have ever been with," or "I love the way you say my name. Say it again, it's Amber." Of course, the conversation becomes more explicit as the minutes fly by. The sad part is that many men believe the women are being honest. A man hooked on a certain woman may call several times a day generating bills up to hundreds of dollars a month.

Operators can make a bigger sale when they can get callers to call back on a private line. The first call, which may have been $5.99 a minute, leads to a private line call at $49.95 for the first three minutes. Incidentally, the operators sometimes "forget" to tell customers about the price increase.

Phone sex defies logic. Men pay for the privilege of talking dirty to a complete stranger who looks nothing like they imagine. If the sexy woman on the other end of the line looked great she would be involved in another aspect of adult entertainment that paid a lot more money.

"Most of the women who worked for that [phone sex] company were poor women or disabled or mothers with kids at home," said Julia who worked as a phone sex operator in New York.[6] Phone sex, however, allows the woman to be and look like whomever she wants. To make matters worse, some of these "women" are actually men. Female or male, they share the ability to create a fantasy that leaves men wanting more.

How do women get involved in the filthy business of phone sex? Most find out about the job through advertisements in local underground newspapers. They call the listed number and leave a recorded message. How they sound in the message helps determine if they get called back.

"Jackie (the supervisor) told me that the job involved 'sexually explicit talk,' and it was 'easy,' and she demonstrated by saying something," said Amy. "There was no training and no official period of observation." Amy described the phone sex room as having six rows of six cubicles, or 36 stations.

Once a woman gets the job as an operator, she will choose a sexy name to use on the phone. According to one phone sex operator, the five basic skills needed are "lying, playing along with offensive fantasies, reading and manipulating a stranger's desire, storytelling, and fearlessly breaking taboos." Lying is number one on the list.

"Lying is a major skill," said Maria, a phone sex operator, "basically going for that person's needs, exactly what they want, and just learning how to be a different person every time. It was difficult at first for me to lie so much, but I got used to it."[7]

The pay rate for a phone sex operator is $6 to $13 an hour.[8] Most are paid as contract employees so the employers avoid paying federal income tax withholding, social security, and workers compensation.[9]

It certainly isn't a glamorous job, so why do women do it? According to one operator, "Looking at everything else that you have to do in L.A., you really have no choice but to work there. Any of the skills I have, they can pay an immigrant $3.00 an hour for. So that is the only thing available to me, and at first it was fun. I sit here, put my feet up. I read a book, I've got my drink, I light a cigarette at my own desk. The phone rings, I talk to some weirdo, say a bunch of stuff, and I get paid 10 bucks an hour — this is great."[10]

I interviewed a woman named Jean who works as a phone sex operator. Of all of my interviews, this one was the most frustrating. She didn't see herself as a phone sex operator who deceived men. She called herself a "counselor." It was hard not to start laughing at her job title.

Counselor? I told her that she advertised in an adult publication and that I suspected that all of her calls were for phone
sex. She never acknowledged my statement but asked me
what degrees I had. Not sure why she asked the question, I
told her that I had a Master's Degree. "I have a Ph.D.," she
boasted, and probably lied. I suppose in her mind the fact
that she had more schooling than me justified her occupation. She never saw the harm she was doing to men and their
families. Poor Jean. Not only was she in the business of
deceiving men, she had also been deceived.

As with all other aspects of pornography and adult
entertainment, phone sex does affect the women involved.
"When I was doing it," said one former phone sex operator,
"I was carrying around all these strange ideas. I'd see men on
the street and think, that man wants to be dominated, or that
man wants to be spanked, or this man wants to beat the s____
out of me. If you have an imagination, and you have the
imagination to do this job, this stuff isn't going to go away."[11]

Another operator said, "I didn't even want to think sex.
Don't talk about sex with me. Don't even touch me, leave
me alone. You get to the point where you do it for 16 hours
a day, you really don't want it in real life, and that's the
truth."[12]

One operator put the men in categories:[13]

> **Candymen** — Guys who ask for fast and
> specific sex acts. They don't stay on the line very
> long but there are many men that fall in this
> category — certainly enough to make it profit-
> able.
>
> **Psychos** — Woman haters and pedophiles.
> An estimated 15 percent of callers fall in this
> category.

"There are some of them that really do hate women,
and that's why they call," said Tamara, "to get out their

frustrations and get girls on the phone. I had one guy that called for me, I'd say seven or eight times, and he was a half-hour caller, and for that half-hour he would want me to cry. He would say, 'I'm gonna beat you, I'm going to whip you' ... and he would beat me up physically, and I just sat there and cried and whimpered and said, 'No, stop, don't rape me, don't do this to me, don't, don't, don't.' "[14]

Gomers — Sad, lonely guys who call to talk to the same woman each time. Calls are not normally sexual in nature. With these guys operators can read magazines, do their nails, or any other mindless activity and just say an occasional, "Oh really?" to keep the caller on line. Gomers will even ask for their hand in marriage.

Goobers — A Gomer gone bad ... where he begins to share his sexual desire with the operator.

"I have had a lot of people, you know, I just tried to be myself," said Charlene, a phone sex operator. "There was this one person, and he was calling me while his girlfriend was out, you know, just to talk to somebody. And it never got explicit sexually, which was nice. Even though he knew he could try. Sometimes you would start out talking and you wouldn't give it to them right away, and they would be really nice, but if you gave it to them, then you couldn't even go back to talking about normal subjects, and it would ruin everything."[15]

Turners — Men who the operators believe could have been dates or boyfriends under different circumstances. They'll often say that this is the first time they have called a phone sex line. They are educated men with good grammar. Operators are sometimes tempted to meet these men.

As you might expect, phone sex operators defend their service by saying that they "help" men with loneliness. "It's a testimony to how continually lonely people are," said Mark. "It's like a drug and you keep looking for that perfect phone call." Mark's search for the perfect call eventually resulted in his getting caught by his wife when she noticed the charge on the credit card statement. Mark is not alone. Many men can tell the same story.

In the end, like every other area of adult entertainment, phone sex no longer satisfies. One male phone sex operator, who disguised himself on the phone as a woman, wrote about one call, "Right after his orgasm, a young caller said to me, 'All this just for this.' I think he was referring to all the trouble it took him to place the call, give out his billing information, and then wait on the line to be connected with a phone sex actress before he could finally (*masturbate*) and have a release that lasts only a few seconds. But that's life."[16] (*Masturbate* was my word since I decided not to use the phrase the phone sex operator used)

The 20th century's greatest tool for communication has been perverted into a tool of destruction. Families lie in the wake of a husband whose sexual fantasies are shared with a woman he will never meet. And it all began by calling a "wrong number."

1 James Lambert, *Porn in America* (Lafayette, LA: Huntington House Publishers, 1997), p. 75.

2 Amy Flowers, *The Fantasy Factory: An Insider's View of the Phone Sex Industry* (Philadelphia, PA: University of Pennsylvania Press, 1998), p. 3.

3 Lambert, *Porn in America*, p. 79.

4 Flowers, *The Fantasy Factory: An Insider's View of the Phone Sex Industry,* p. 5.

5 Gary Anthony with Rocky Bennett, *Dirty Talk: Diary of a Phone-Sex Mistress* (Amherst, NY: Prometheus Books, 1998), p. 37.

6 Wendy Chapkis, *Live Sex Acts — Women Performing Erotic Labor* (New York: Routledge, 1997), p. 111.

7 Flowers, *The Fantasy Factory: An Insider's View of the Phone Sex Industry,* p. 17–18, 46, 48.
8 Lambert, *Porn in America*, p. 79.
9 Flowers, *The Fantasy Factory: An Insider's View of the Phone Sex Industry,* p. 14.
10 Ibid., p. 29.
11 Lambert, *Porn in America*, p. 80.
12 Flowers, *The Fantasy Factory: An Insider's View of the Phone Sex Industry,* p. 57.
13 Ibid., p. 66.
14 Ibid.
15 Ibid., p. 80.
16 Anthony and Bennett, *Dirty Talk, Diary of a Phone-Sex Mistress*, p. 329.

9

The Internet —— The Brave New World of Porn

For why should you, my son, be exhilarated with an adulteress, and embrace the bosom of a foreigner? For the ways of a man are before the eyes of the Lord, and He watches all his paths (Prov. 5:20–21).

MY WIFE, KATHY, TOOK A MEAL to a sick friend. As they visited for a while, her friend said that her sister's husband had confessed to being addicted to pornography on the Internet. The wife was shocked and deeply hurt. The marriage is in trouble now with a bleak future. I don't know this woman's name, but I know there are many more like her. Some sit in church pews with husbands who are elders and deacons in the church. Others sit near the front of the church and look up at their husband as he preaches another sermon. Christian men are not immune to the troubles found on the Internet.

An Ann Landers column recently caught my eye with

a letter from a woman who had a problem with her husband. "My husband and I have a fabulous marriage," the letter began. "We have two wonderful children, ages 22 and 25. 'Phil' has a lucrative career that allows us to indulge our mutual love to travel. Our friends see us as a close, affectionate, and devoted couple. Here's the problem. 'Phil' has become obsessed with porn on the Internet. When he first started to spend a lot of time on the computer in the middle of the night and early morning, he told me it was 'research.' I walked in on him one morning and caught him looking at some very provocative girlie stuff. He said it was a matter of curiosity. When I took a closer look at what he was watching, it made me sick. He was embarrassed and promised to stop, and I believe he meant it."[1] The letter concluded in the next paragraph and you can guess how it ended? That's right, his promise didn't last. Her husband was addicted to porn on the Internet.

The letter saddened me since she began by saying that they had a "fabulous marriage." A husband addicted to pornography on the Internet fell short of my definition of "fabulous." She also said that their friends see them as "close, affectionate and devoted." I doubt God has the same opinion.

Of all the sources of pornography and adult entertainment, the Internet concerns me most. According to the anti-pornography group Enough Is Enough, the Internet is the fastest-growing distribution channel for illegal pornography.[2] The number of personal computers hooked up to the Internet jumped to 82 million in 1997, an amazing 71 percent increase according to Dataquest Inc., a California market research firm.[3] It is expected to triple to 268 million by the year 2001. That's a lot of people! Unfortunately, more people equal more moneymaking schemes involving pornography. The problem with Internet porn will continue to get worse as technology gets better.

The number of sexually explicit sites are estimated to

be in the hundreds of thousands according to Kelly Haggerty, product marketing manager at ELRON, a company that sells a program to track employee's Internet use.[4] It's big business that clogs the Internet every night.

People are looking for porn sites and they are easy to find. According to the *Washington Post*, the top ten words used for searching the Internet in 1998 were:[5]

1. free	6. XXX
2. sex	7. Diana
3. nude	8. pics
4. pictures	9. new
5. warez	10. university

Cyberspace porn sites are making big money. The *Washington Post* estimated that adult sites generated an estimated one billion dollars in revenue annually.[6]

Often the temptation to view Internet porn comes without looking for it. When I became the chaplain at Interstate Batteries, I told Kathy, one of my team members, that I wanted to get speakers for my computer. She offered me a set she wasn't using. When I hooked them up I tried to find a Christian radio station on the Internet to see if they worked. Using the word "Christian" for my search, I found over 20 pages of sites to look through. I also had a problem. At the top of the page was an advertising banner, which are common on the Internet. The banner contained the head-shot of a beautiful, unblemished woman with inviting eyes and a smile that could melt an ice sculpture in the Arctic. The advertisement was for the *High Society Free Sex Tour*. At the right of the banner was a scroll down button.

As Kathy looked over my shoulder we were both dumbfounded. My search word was not "sex," it was "Christian." Although my intention was pure, a lustful picture was staring me in the face. When I hit the scroll bar to see what else was on the banner (a bad move) I made another discovery. It didn't scroll — it went directly to the porn site. Here I was the new chaplain at Interstate Batteries, with a married female co-worker looking over my shoulder, and I was in a porn site. Shocked and embarrassed, I must have set a record for the shortest visit to a porn site.

Of course, this was a temptation that was easily defeated. In fact, it was not a temptation at all. The very thought of entering a porn site as a chaplain with a woman looking over my shoulder was inconceivable. The situation, however, might be different if I was at home working on my computer at night with my family sound asleep upstairs. If I searched for the word "Christian" and saw the Free Sex Tour provided by High Society, what would I do? I hope I would exit the site as I did at work. But it angers me that I have to deal with a temptation I never sought. On-line porn is a big problem with a huge following.

To make matters worse, porn sites have received free advertising in the media. In July 1998, major newspapers and radio stations contained information about a new site that would show two 18-year-old virgins being "deflowered." The press release boasted that the company that brought us the Pamela Anderson-Tommy Lee "honeymoon" would provide us this latest treat. From July 18 until the big day on August 4, Internet users around the world could monitor the progress of this young couple.

"We have decided to help Mike and Diane achieve maximum exposure for their daring initiation to sexual enjoyment because we are so passionate about freedom of expression," said Seth Warshavsky, president and CEO of Internet Entertainment Group. "In its own way, this is a perfect example of how the First Amendment works, and we are proud to be a part of it through this beautiful moment in Internet history."[7]

Oh, please. The only thing IEG is passionate about is debauchery and profit. Warshavsky called it a beautiful moment. God calls it sin. The site was later discontinued, not because it was indecent, but because IEG learned that the couple never planned on following through with their act of "love." IEG was upset about the deception. Imagine that — pornographers upset about deception. Is it possible the pot is calling the kettle black?

IEG was later involved in plastering nude photos of radio talk show counselor Dr. Laura Schlessinger on the Internet. Touted as the "Dirty Dozen," these photos were taken by a former mentor and friend of Dr. Laura back in the 1970s. According to the *San Jose Mercury News*, hundreds of thousands of visitors went to the site in a ten-hour period. The response to the photos was a feeding frenzy of depraved and addicted men who find lustful excitement at the expense of a woman's shame.

Unbelievably, Judge Dean Pregerson of the U.S. District Court Central District of California ruled that IEG would not be restrained from showing the nude and semi-nude photos. "We are delighted at Judge Pregerson's decision," said Warshavsky, who called the decision a "victory for freedom and truth." "We never doubted our legal right to put the photos and story on the web." Not surprisingly, Warshavsky cares nothing of his moral responsibility. In our sex-starved culture, I suppose nothing should shock us any longer.

VICTORIA NO LONGER HAS A SECRET

Countless American men were glued to the television set during the 1999 Super Bowl between the Denver Broncos and Atlanta Falcons. In recent years the Super Bowl has become famous for incredible commercials. Not only is the winner decided on the football field, but also the advertising winner is declared in the media the following morning.

In 1999 there was a new contestant to the Super Bowl advertising game. It was Victoria's Secret. Their Super Bowl commercial was an ad for their February 3 fashion show that included super models wearing sexy lingerie.

Men and boys alike watching the Super Bowl got an eye-full as Victoria's Secret gave the audience a preview of things to come.

Victoria's Secret expected a good turn-out to their on-line fashion show, anticipating 250,000 to 500,000 web users.[8] Boy, were they in for a surprise! Some estimates reported 1.5 million people fighting to get in. Am I to assume these were all women in need of underwear?

"The success of our marketing campaign . . . exceeded our wildest dreams," said Ed Razek, president of brand and creative services for Intimate Brands, Inc., parent company of Victoria's Secret.[9] Unfortunately, not everyone would agree. Many people could not get in and those who could saw fuzzy images of scantily clad models during the 17-minute show.

"If you got on, what you saw were grainy breasts," said *Wired* magazine contributing editor David Bennahum. "It looked like amateur porn with really good-looking women."[10] Was the fashion show about lingerie or lust? While Victoria's Secret failed to produce a quality on-line show, I doubt they'll pack their bags and go home. I suspect they won't make the same mistake next time. In the future you can be sure that Victoria's Secret will be ready for the onslaught of men looking to fulfill their lusts.

"I'm one lucky guy to be here," said model Edward McMahon who was in the live audience. "They're beautiful ladies wearing barely nothing, and they make every man's dream come true."[11] Every man? Hardly. My dream woman is not a grainy woman found on-line. She is the one I promised to love, honor, and cherish . . . till death do us part.

ON-LINE PORN IS NO SECRET

Who keeps on-line porn sites in business? "Entrepreneurs, executives, financial people. They have money, they have the right computers and Internet connections, and they are often lonely and alienated," said one successful adult-entertainment businessman.[12]

It has been difficult for lawmakers to apply decency standards out of fear of infringing on First Amendment rights. Of course, we don't seem to have a problem with the damage it is doing to children and families.

When a man is struggling with pornography, there are usually obstacles to fulfilling his lust. If he goes into a convenience store to buy a magazine, he has to face the clerk as he makes the purchase. What happens if someone from the PTA or his church walks in as he reaches for the magazine? The same holds true for video stores.

There are no obstacles for a man searching for pornography on the Internet. He can search all he wants in the "comfort" of his own home.

Richard has a beautiful wife and five children. He also teaches a Bible study on Monday nights. A few nights a week he sends his family off to bed as he works on his Sunday school lesson. As soon as he feels the family is sound asleep, he begins his search for hard-core pornography.

"It's too easy to find," said Richard. "Once I get started, it's difficult trying to stop. My intentions are normally good when I get started, but once my family is asleep, it's as if I feel a pull from the computer. I hate what I'm doing and feel like a horrible hypocrite. I know I'll eventually get caught and it will devastate my wife, yet I can't stop."

The popularity of sex on the Internet grows daily. An editorial in the *New York Post* reported, "The dirty little secret of the Internet isn't so little, but it is very dirty. The Internet is, to some degree, dedicated to pornography." Pornography on the Internet is much worse than what you would find in a *Playboy* magazine. Images include bestiality, genital piercing, sexual torture, urination, and defecation.

It's an issue that computer magazines can hardly avoid. "Admit it," writes Chris O'Malley for *Verge* magazine.

"The first time you logged on the Internet you went straight to the porn web sites — out of curiosity, of course. Okay, maybe it was the second time. But you went there, well, because you could. With a few clicks of your mouse, you could have pictures, videos, 900 numbers, really graphic weird stuff, right there in your den, inches from your nose, on your computer screen. In a way, it was like sneaking a peek at Dad's dog-eared copy of *Playboy* when you were a kid." The article continued by giving "twenty enlightening web sites that could teach you a thing or two — or three."[13]

I know the addresses of many hard-core porn sites, but there is no way I would ever include them in anything I wrote. The reason is simple. If men are given the addresses of the web sites, many will take a peek for themselves. I suspect many of the readers of O'Malley's article did exactly that.

I spoke at a church men's retreat on the subject of pornography and one of the leaders was explaining how dangerous the Internet can be. He explained how he had inadvertently found a hard-core porn site while searching for something else. He said the site was horrible. He then gave out the web address. I shook my head knowing that on Sunday night, some of the men would look at the site "to see how bad it really was."

A typical porn site begins with a black background with the word "ENTER" in a bright neon color. When you enter there is a warning about what lies ahead and several statements you must agree to before you can proceed further.

> I understand that _____ offers a variety of sexually explicit materials for adult entertainment and I do not find sexual material, written, graphic, or otherwise, to be offensive or objectionable.
>
> I am at least 18 years of age and have the legal

right to possess adult material in my community.

I understand the standards and laws of the community to which I am transporting this material, and am solely responsible for my actions.

All material I transport from this site is for my own personal use, and will not be reused in any manner.

I agree to respect the copyrights of the owners of the material I find on _____.

My interest in this material is personal, and not professional.

I suppose those statements free them from legal responsibility. My, how convenient. Sites may have a titillating graphic on the warning screen that does more to entice than to discourage. I suspect few turn back at this point. It's not a warning — it's an advertisement.

The next screen gives you the opportunity to join. Of course, you'll need your credit card handy. Hmm ... so you don't want to join right away? Well, what you need is a free preview! Every site has that, too.

Previews vary. Some have thumbnail pictures that are difficult to see. Others have larger pictures that are slightly blurred. Still more are clear but the genitals are covered with something from a black box to a flame. Finally, some pictures are clear and large, but low in quantity. Once you've seen the preview, it's time to make the decision about what to do with your credit card. Many men search aimlessly for free previews, hoping to find enough to satisfy their lust.

Pornographers don't mind if you do that because they know once you are addicted, you'll pull out that credit card and join. It's just a matter of time.

Some on-line porn sites have a free trial membership that you can cancel when the trial is over. Canceling is not as easy as it sounds. The Better Business Bureau for the Southern California counties of Los Angeles, Orange, and

Riverside logged 62 complaints in a two-year period about one such site that wouldn't stop charging credit cards. The bureau's file said consumers "reported they attempted to cancel repeatedly via e-mail requests, phone, letter . . . their cancellation requests were allegedly not acknowledged by the company."[14]

Jane Duvall, who has an on-line sex guide, knows why companies get away with it. "Everybody looks at porn . . . if more people admitted it, they'd be able to go to their credit card company and say, 'Hey, I'm being ripped off.' " A big part of the on-line adult business is getting money from people who don't want to admit that they look at it."[15]

It seems the shame is so great that some men would rather get ripped off than admit they have paid for on-line porn. How sad.

As you might suspect, *Playboy* has its own website with over 18,600 subscribers and an average of 4.7 million hits in one seven-day period.[16] On a site owned by former Bill Clinton mistress Gennifer Flowers, callers talk to models who use handheld cameras to beam live photographs of themselves doing whatever the caller requests. The service costs $9.95 to enroll and $5.95 a minute for one woman. Flowers defends her site calling it "cute and amusing." I wonder how many wives of addicted husbands are laughing with her. It should not be surprising that sales in the adult entertainment sector on the Internet is surpassed only by sales of computer products and travel.[17]

Video conferencing sites, which are a mix of phone sex and a live club, are growing in cyberspace. These sites allow customers to hook up with private laptop dancers and exchange written messages. Oh, did I mention you had to be a credit card-holding customer? Most charge by the minute but a few offer monthly fees. One such site charges $49.95 for 30 minutes.

Full time dancers in video conferencing may earn in the ballpark of $70,000 a year with health benefits. Gary Mittman, the founder of one such site, boasts revenues of over $1 million a month.

In addition to money, the dancers see other benefits as well. "No drunks," said Sterling, a former strip club dancer who now dances on-line. Sterling's company has grown to over 75 dancers working in studios in San Diego and Las Vegas. Other studios are being built in Amsterdam, Prague, and Japan.[18] Business is good.

Most porn sites on the Internet consist of pictures . . . and plenty of them. One of the web's largest sites offers its 55,000 members more than 10,000 sexually explicit images and adds almost 1,000 a month. While *Playboy* and *Penthouse* own web sites, most are owned by individuals. Beth, a struggling accountant in Washington, wondered how she would put her children through college. This self-described "family oriented person" decided to try her hand at on-line porn. She grossed over $900,000 a year.

"I never expected there would be income like this," said Beth. "The first checks were more money in a week than I made in a month."[19]

Many operators start out just for the "fun" of it, not expecting to make any money. Ricquie, a 29-year-old mother of two, said she started her site with her husband for fun. "My husband finds it exciting to see me on the page."[20] Initially, she had four or five photographs posted but now she has included racier pictures with a subscription service.

A former exotic dancer named Danni also owns a popular site. "You're always getting this message that you're wasting your life, that it's a dead end. And that's not true," she said. "I know lots of models who have become agents or created their own video companies. Me, I built a web site."[21] Danni grosses over $2.5 million a year. She sadly is running toward a dead end with reckless abandon, grieving the heart of God.

Porn-site operators see it as big business. It shouldn't come as any surprise since almost 30 percent of Americans on the Internet visit adult web sites in a month. "If it was No. 2 pencils people wanted to see," said one proprietor named Glenn Grattiano, "I'd have nice yellow streaks going across the screen. But sex sells. Look at advertising, television, movies. It's the way of the world."[22] Yes, and it's Satan's world.

Pornographers like Grattiano are in the business to make a profit by feeding the lusts of men. They don't care about you or your family. We have to stop hitting their sites. Pornographers cannot stay in business if they don't make money. If you have a problem with on-line porn, get on your knees right now and ask God to give you the strength to be victorious.

Unfortunately, porn addiction follows many men to work where they typically have free, unsupervised Internet access. The top non-business-related sites visited most frequently by companies with Internet access are sexually explicit sites, almost doubling PointCast, the second place finisher.

According to a *New York Times* article, 100 companies tested software to find out what employees were hitting on the Internet. Of those companies, 68 had employees hitting on-line pornography. "Some companies had ten pages of inappropriate addresses," said Kelly Haggerty, from ELRON.[23]

While some companies are making efforts to restrict employee access to sexually explicit sites, many men's addictions drive them to view porn sites during work hours, even at the risk of losing their jobs.

"In every training program I've done in the last year, the issue of surfing the Net and sexually explicit visuals has come up," said Trisha Brinkman, a consultant to corporations about sexual harassment.[24] According to the National Coalition for the Protection of Children and Families, the *Penthouse* web site was visited 12,823 times in a one-month period by employees at IBM, Apple Computer, and AT&T.[25]

During a two-week audit at the Pacific Northwest National Laboratory, 98 employees were caught entering adult sites during office hours. Twenty-one were suspended and the others received a written reprimand.[26] One computer company in Houston dismissed 20 employees, each of whom had logged more than 1,000 hits on sexually explicit web sites.[27] Six employees at Electronic Data Systems in Troy, Michigan, were fired for visiting adult sites. One of those fired included a respected systems administrator who hit the same sexually explicit web site 15,000 times in one month.[28] The list of companies could go on and on.

Robert, who was married with four children, lost his job as a result of his addiction to Internet porn at the office. The first time he was caught he was called into his supervisor's office and given a reprimand and warned that he could be fired for future abuses.

"I just couldn't control it," Robert said. "With Internet access, suddenly there was this wealth of material that I could get easily — and for free." Robert is not alone. According to *PC World*, repeated visits to adult sites are the most common cause for Internet-related job dismissals.[29]

Pornography on the Internet is out of control and countless men are trapped, even at the risk of losing all they hold dear. And the problem with the Internet does not end with pictures, videos, and video conferencing. It gets worse with one word — cybersex.

Cybersex chat rooms are packed every hour of the day. According to Jack Rickard of *Boardwatch Magazine*, at least 50,000 people are chatting on 500 to 700 "sex talk" lines each day.[30] Some are men late at night whose family has gone to bed hours earlier. Others are men at work who take a break from the action of a busy day. Cybersex chat rooms, the playground of the 1990s, attract young and old, married and single, people of every color and creed.

In weak moments, I suspect most men have pictured themselves involved in encounters that they would never actually participate in. Cybersex allows the imagination to run wild. Press a few buttons and you can be anyone you want to be. An over-40, overweight businessman who was never considered handsome, even by his own parents, can be a 27-year-old bodybuilder who is the spitting image of Tom Cruise. Some men even take on female personalities who look great in two-piece bathing suits. On-line, you can lead a double, triple, and quadruple life. Your personalities are only limited by your imagination.

One Christian man said this about his cybersex experience: "I had been a subscriber to a popular computer on-line service for about six weeks when I saw an announcement to try out the romance connection chat rooms. I thought to myself, *Why not?* I clicked on the appropriate icon, and there I was in the midst of a room with 23 other people. I scrolled through the screen names of several participants, picked out one that resembled a female name. Over the next 20 minutes we led each other through a fantasy date that ended up with our having sex on the floor."[31] Over the next three hours he had cybersex with ten different women.

After confessing his sin to God he later went back to erase his pseudo-name only to enter again with a *female* name. He was bombarded by instant messages from men. "Out of curiosity I went along with them," he said. "Some were very up-front and graphic about having cybersex; others were more subtle and polite. After that session I became very disgusted with myself."[32]

Cybersex entices people to live out their wildest fantasy with no contact, no disease, no relationship, no problems. How wonderfully simple. And how deceptive.

In a chat room I asked "Sally" how her husband felt about her desire to engage in cybersex. "It's not like it's real so he doesn't mind," she informed me. I had the funny feeling "Sally" was a man. Two out of three "women" in chat rooms are believed by many to be men. One "lonely housewife" told me her husband traveled a lot and she was looking for another woman to have cybersex with. Hmm . . . sounded fishy to me. Men masquerading as women — think about that the next time you are tempted to find "love" in a chat room.

Chat rooms are addictive and keep many men up late at night. They provide a web of perverted fantasy which distances and isolates men from genuine, flesh and blood intimacy with the people in their lives.

Chat rooms are also breeding grounds for pedophiles. In September 1999, the executive vice-president for a major Internet search engine was arrested for attempting to meet a 13-year-old girl in Santa Monica, California. His job was to oversee e-mail and chat rooms. According to court papers, he told the girl to skip school so they could meet and have her strip naked for him. Sadly, his story is not unique.

If you've never been in a chat room, don't even explore the possibility. Chat rooms are like Lay's Potato Chips — you won't have just one. You'll go back again.

Now that you understand the problem, here are some practical things you can do in your home to protect yourself.

Keep the computer in a room with a door that can't be locked. A man tempted by porn on the Internet should never be on the computer with the door locked. Anyone in the family should have access to the room where the computer is located.

Have the computer screen face the door. Many men have become quite proficient at changing screens in an instant. The risk is greater when the screen is facing the door. Knowing that someone could enter the room and see what they have on the computer may serve as a deterrent.

Don't work on the computer after your family has gone to bed. This one is critical. Most men struggle late at night when the family is asleep.

Chat rooms and porn sites are packed after hours. The risk is too great. Turn in when your wife goes to bed. If you think you can handle the Internet after hours, you are probably in trouble. I would also recommend setting a limit on the number of hours you use the computer in your home.

When I was on the radio program "Point of View" with Kerby Anderson, I told the male listeners about not being on the Internet after the family had gone to bed. I recommended turning in when their wife goes to bed. The very first phone call we got was from a man who said we had "gone off the deep end." Ouch. This was my first time on national radio, answering my first call, and this guy told me I had gone off the deep end. I was stunned. Sensing my dilemma and noticing that no words were coming out of my mouth, Kerby masterfully debated the guy while I collected my thoughts. "Do I think every man in America needs to go to bed when his wife goes to bed?" I replied. "Certainly not. But if a man struggles with sexual temptation, he'd better. Yes, I stand by my statement." Guys, it's all about being in places where we can fall. Sexual temptation and late night activities don't mix well. I learned that lesson the hard way.

Find a wholesome server. We all know about AOL and CompuServe. Both have many wonderful features, but I believe both are dangerous for the man struggling with sexual temptation. Look for other servers that block out sexually explicit sites. Sure, they are far from perfect, but it is much harder to find porn sites on cleaner servers. Integrity On-Line and ifriendly.com block offensive sites they know about. Users help keep the servers clean by reporting offensive sites.

Install blocking software. Software to block offensive sites is available for purchase at any

computer store. I believe that Christian men should
never get on the Internet at home if it is not
protected. The temptation is too great. Even with
blocking software and a wholesome server, pornographers are too sharp to let that stop them.
They will do whatever it takes to get you hooked.
Fortunately, there is software that can help you.
Just check your local computer store.

And guys . . . one more thing. Let your *wife* install the
blocking software. If she installs it, you can't take it off in a
weak moment. Having your wife install the software is not
about trust. It's about protection. It's about a wife recogniz-
ing the danger to her husband and caring enough to help him
protect himself. If my wife received a free catalog from
Victoria's Secret, I know she would get rid of it before I got
home. She wants to help me make righteous decisions. She
wants me to be a man of God. I need her help. I don't have
to worry about fleeing from temptation if there is no temptation. It just makes sense. Don't be stubborn and resent the
fact that your wife has access that you don't. Guys, that's
pride. Get over it.

Get involved. Do you know what Congress is
doing about porn on the Internet? They need to
know that you are concerned about decency issues, especially pertaining to the Internet. You
probably have a local decency office in your city.
Give them a call and ask what you can do to help.
Decency is everyone's business.

In the workplace you can get involved in helping
yourself and other men by talking to your computer folks
about using ELRON Internet Manager or WEBSENSE.
Both do a great job at identifying employees who visit
inappropriate sites. Knowing that the company can monitor

Internet usage is a major deterrent for many men.

Porn on the Internet has one motive — to exploit your weakness for profit. "Porn comes down to this," said porn-site operator Hester Nash of Los Angeles, "We women are exploiting men's weaknesses. You're handing me your credit card. I'm not a victim. I'm exploiting you!"[33] She sounds proud of herself for the destruction she is causing.

She's right about the exploitation, but she is as much a victim as the addicted man. When you play the game of pornography, there is enough defeat for everyone. It's a game that creates losers.

Sadly, Nash does not see the consequences. "I don't think I'm doing anything wrong," she boasts, "but I don't want to make myself a target or have Jerry Falwell banging on my door."[34] She needs to be concerned about more than Jerry Falwell. One day she'll be in the presence of God.

 1 Ann Landers column, "Husband Is Addicted to Pornography on the Internet," *Dallas Morning News*, May 22, 1998.
 2 "The Tough Task of Defining What's Too Explicit to Be Seen," *USA Today*, August 19, 1997.
 3 Donna Rice-Hughes, *Kids Online — Protecting Your Children in Cyberspace* (Grand Rapids, MI: Revell, 1998), p. 22.
 4 "Keeping Track of Employee's Online Voyeurism," *New York Times*, May 7, 1998.
 5 Rice-Hughes, *Kids Online,* p. 64.
 6 Ibid., p. 53.
 7 Press release, Internet Entertainment Group, July 17, 1998.
 8 "Victoria's Secret Show: Guess You Had to Be There," *Philadelphia Online, The Inquirer*, February 5, 1999.
 9 "Victoria's Secret Web Show Draws Record Crowd," *San Francisco Examiner*, February 4, 1999.
10 "It's Just Bra, Humbug — Victoria's Secret Show Netlocked," *New York Daily News*, February 4, 1999.
11 "Secret Webcast May Net a Million Viewers," *New York Post*, February 4, 1999.
12 Paul Franson, "The Net's Dirty Little Secret: Sex Sells," *Upside Magazine*, April 1998.

13 Chris O'Malley, "Looking for Sex," *Verge*, Spring 1997.
14 Steve Silberman, "Porn Patrons Billed, Unfulfilled," *Wired News*, May 19, 1998.
15 Ibid.
16 Rice-Hughes, *Kids Online*, p. 53.
17 Ibid.
18 "Erotic Dancers Shimmy into Cyberspace," *USA Today*, July 3, 1996.
19 "Sex Sites Hot on the Web," *USA Today*, August 19, 1997.
20 Franson, "The Net's Dirty Little Secret: Sex Sells."
21 "Sex Sites Hot on the Web," *USA Today*.
22 Ibid.
23 "Keeping Track of Employee's On-Line Voyeurism," *New York Times*.
24 "Cyberspace Sex Causes Problems for Companies," *Dallas Morning News*, August 14, 1996.
25 "Pornography in the Workplace," National Coalition for the Protection of Children and Families.
26 Ibid.
27 "Cyberspace Sex Causes Problems for Companies," *Dallas Morning News*.
28 "The Web and Your Business," *PC World*, November 1997.
29 Ibid.
30 "Facts about Pornography," American Family Association.
31 Robert Daniels, *The War Within* (Wheaton, IL: Crossway Books, 1997), p. 200.
32 Ibid., p. 201.
33 "Sex Site Owners Urge Caution," *USA Today*, August 19, 1997.
34 Ibid.

10

A Place for "Gentlemen"

Keep your way far from her, and do not go near the door of her house (Prov. 5:8).

AS I MENTIONED IN CHAPTER 1, I am no stranger to Gentlemen's Clubs . . . excuse me, let's call them what they are, sexually oriented businesses (SOBs). In the late 1970s I visited every SOB in Columbus, Georgia, several times. When I was transferred to Fort Hood, Texas, a friend and I would go to an SOB in Austin on weekends.

Killeen, the city adjacent to Fort Hood, had many clubs, too. We never went to those clubs because we did not want to be seen by soldiers under our command. I suppose we had a strange kind of morality. Weekends in Austin were either spent attempting to pick up women at a country-western club or watching women strip for money at an SOB.

Shortly after being reassigned to Fort Benning, Georgia, I met my wife, so my days at the clubs came to an end, or so I thought. A few years later I was sent to Fort Leavenworth, Kansas, for the Combined Arms and Services Staff School on an unaccompanied assignment that lasted three months.

One Saturday night I went out to dinner with a group of ten other army officers to Kansas City. The meal was great and we enjoyed spending time together. As we walked toward the cars at the end of the evening, one of the guys had a great idea. Why not all go to a club and watch women strip? Although I was not a Christian at the time, instantly a battle was raging inside me. My morality told me those places were for single men. I had been happily married for over two years. It wasn't for me and I knew it.

I had a problem, however. We had ten guys in two cars and no one else said they thought it was a bad idea. How could I spoil the evening for everyone else? I rationalized away my silence in a matter of minutes. Once inside the club, I looked at the women and enjoyed myself as much as the guy who made the suggestion.

As soon as I got back to Fort Leavenworth, well after midnight, I was overcome with guilt. The next morning I called Kathy and told her what I had done. I asked for her forgiveness. She said she understood the situation I was in and forgave me. I knew I had hurt her though, and I hated that feeling. With the exception of research visits with Dallas vice officers, I have not been back to an SOB since.

Later I wondered if any of the other guys made similar calls to their wives. Was it possible that there were other men who did not want to betray their marriage vows by lusting after another woman? Maybe there was another guy hoping someone else would speak up. Who knows, maybe the guy who made the suggestion was the only one who wanted to go. What the situation needed that night was a man committed to his wife in word and deed, a man who would stand up and say, "Guys, that's not for me. I'd rather go home and call my wife." That man should have been me.

Making the call was difficult. Was it possible that my wife of two years would feel that I no longer desired her? Would she be concerned that this was the first of many sexual indiscretions on my part? Although my words communicated my devotion to her, my actions communicated lustful desires that could have easily weakened our marriage bond. I took a horrible risk — all because I did not have the courage to say no. I deceived myself into believing that speaking up would ruin the evening for the other guys. The truth is that my silence caused the greatest ruin.

I had to make the telephone call to my wife, however, to stop the deception. I knew I didn't want to ever return to a sexually oriented business. It was time to come clean to the woman I loved.

Over the years I have learned about the power of deception that has found a breeding ground in sexually oriented businesses. Deception runs wild when lust is out of control. As I mentioned earlier, there is enough deception to go around for everyone. In my days in adult entertainment, I was both the deceiver and the deceived. Both roles are very destructive.

DECEIVING THE WIVES

The ones I feel for the most are the wives who are waiting for their husbands to come home. Men give a variety of excuses to cover their tracks. Working late, going out with the guys — the excuses are numerous. While some men tell their wives where they are going, many do not. I believe the deception is highest among Christian men since they have more to lose if they are found out.

"My old lady would kill me if she knew I did this every other week," said Charlie, a regular at a strip club. "After a while it costs a lot of money. But it's better than having a mistress. I may be on a diet, but I like to read the menu."[1] Poor Charlie. Little does he know that the "items" on his menu will lead to marriage poisoning — poisoning caused by deception.

When I spoke to Jack he confided that he went to a sexually oriented business for the first time in many years. "I took time off from work and just stopped in for no reason.

I ended up spending four hours in the club and wasted over $100. When I left I reeked of cigarette smoke so I went home and showered and changed clothes before my wife got home. I was so afraid she would know that I did something wrong." For Jack, the lie had begun. He was not caught and now feels a tremendous temptation to return to the birthplace of his deception.

DECEIVING THE MEN

Of the people being deceived, the men are the most gullible. They don't want reality, they want deception! Reality is what is waiting for them at home. In the world of pornography and adult entertainment, many men are seeking an escape. They come to an industry that is very willing to please. The deception for the men is twofold. Not only are they deceived by the dancers, they also deceive themselves.

"A man comes here because this is a place where he doesn't have to be a husband or a daddy," said Aimee, a 25-year-old dancer. "He can be whatever he wants. Some build themselves up to be millionaires or CIA agents. We just pretend to believe them."[2] Dancers are more than willing to buy into their temporary fantasy world filled with deception. It is their greatest role.

Dancers deceive men for one reason — money. Many clubs have even added ATM machines just in case some guy forgets to bring enough cash. A cat and mouse game is played to see who gets what they want first. Unfortunately, it is a game that no one wins.

ESKIMOS, WOLVES, AND DECEPTION

Radio personality Paul Harvey told a gruesome story about how an Eskimo uses deception to kill a wolf. First he coats his knife blade with animal blood and allows it to freeze. Additional layers are added until the blade is completely covered by frozen blood. The Eskimo fixes the knife in the ground with the blade pointing up. The wolf follows his nose to the bait and licks it slowly. Tasting the fresh frozen blood he begins to lick faster, lapping the blade until the keen edge is bare. Harder and harder he licks the sharp blade.

His craving is so great that he doesn't notice the sting of the blade on his own tongue. The wolf does not realize that his thirst is now being satisfied by his *own* blood. His appetite wants more and more until he is eventually found dead in the snow.

The wolf doesn't want to see the pain that lies behind the frozen blood. The man who has given into addiction doesn't want to see the pain that lies behind his lust. That's deception.

IT'S ALL IN A NAME

I never met with a dancer who danced using the name given to her at birth. Amber, Country, Olivia, Candy . . . the list goes on. The names are changed in an effort to deceive. Sure, the men are deceived because this woman is not who she claims to be.

Many of the names are suggestive in an effort to attract business and retain customers. With the name and the look, combined with erotic dancing, men are deceived. They believe things about these women that are just not true.

WHAT YOU SEE IS WHAT YOU GET?

Heidi began dancing while in college and she quickly learned about the deception. "It's just a few inches of skin, but the way these men react you'd think I was a goddess or movie star. I walked around the ring, smiling and thinking what fools they were."[3] Seeing dancers parting with their clothing is all part of the deception. As they dance eye contact is made as if to communicate the message that *you* have a chance with her. When the dancer joins the man at the table, he is thinking about sex and she is thinking about money. Each deceives the other to achieve their goal.

Men are also deceived by the appearance of the woman. Approximately 80 percent of the women in adult entertainment get breast implants. There are many doctors who are more than happy to facilitate the deception.

Dr. Patrick Graham, a plastic surgeon in southern Florida, says that 6 out of 15 breast enhancement surgeries he performs each month are on strippers. For those who don't have the cash, the American Society of Plastic and Reconstructive Surgeons will offer a two-year payment plan at 14 to 24 percent interest. My, how convenient! Other women will have men, called "sugar daddies," pay for their breast enhancement surgery.[4] No, these are not daddies who love and care for them. They are part of the pain, abuse, and deception.

Searching for the look that sells, many women go to great expense to deceive. "I used to get my hair done every two weeks — $100 every two weeks," said Dakota. "I get a pair of shoes every other week when I work a lot. They wear out, and they don't have enough support. When I'm dancing and I'm drinking, I'm stepping on my own feet. Once a month I need all new makeup. When I used to buy good makeup, I spent $300."[5] Overall, Dakota said she spent $1,000 a month to look good for her customers, all in an effort to deceive.

Costs vary, but for an upscale club the chart below provides a look at "typical" expenses for strippers as they try to become women they are not:

Items and cost
Liposuction — $1,000 per site
Breast implants — $4,500–$7,000
Lip enhancements — $2,500
Hair — $5/ night to club stylist, $200/month to a
    hairdresser
Tanning — $50 a month
Sculptured nails — $100 a month

Shoes — $100 a pair, three pairs a month
Wardrobe, gowns — 25 gowns at $100 each
Wardrobe, negligees/ lingerie — $50–$75 each

Strippers depend on their bodies and their ability to separate men from the money in their wallets. "A lot of guys don't know that they have been hustled until they walk out the door missing two or three hundred dollars," said Danny.[6]

Club owners help the dancers create an environment of deception. Some owners even offer helpful hints. Former club owner Michael Peter required dancers to read his employee handbook, which offered the following advice:

Three Things to Remember:
Sit down and introduce yourself. This is like foreplay and capture's the guests undivided attention.

The dance is like the sexual act itself. It should be sensual and moving and leave the guest breathless.

Leaving the guest immediately following the dance is like rolling over and going to sleep. Stay for a few minutes, maybe smoke a cigarette, and let your guest enjoy the glow he will feel after your dance.

Peter also lists "unspeakable acts":[7]

1. Don't talk about last night.
2. Don't talk about company matters.
3. Don't talk about other guests.
4. Don't discuss politics, religion, or racial subjects.
5. Don't get personal.
6. Don't get smart.
7. Avoid the appearance of giving orders to guests.
8. Don't complain, gripe, rant, or rave.

9. Don't argue.
10. Don't embarrass guests by correcting them.
11. Don't talk about yourself.

Wow — 11 "unspeakable acts" on his list. It made me wonder if Michael Peter ever looked at God's list which He called the Ten Commandments. If Peter ever takes the time to do that, he'll find his business on the list. Peter's rules, however, were developed to hide the true identity of the dancers. Men don't want to see the pain and abuse behind the mask. They want to believe the deception.

DECEIVING THE DANCER

Tragically, the dancers know the pain of deception. Like the men, they often deceive themselves. "I close my eyes and pretend I'm in another world," said Shanelle, a stripper in southern Florida.[8] The dancers live in a world of pain and abuse, yet they portray a world of seduction and sexual fulfillment. To survive, most dancers must buy into the lies and some actually begin to believe them. "As a topless dancer, I always felt like a temple dancer," said Marion. "I had an unbridled spirit that seemed to convey to men, 'I'm a beautiful woman, I know it, I am not ashamed of my body, I have nothing to hide.' Such confidence has a refreshing effect on the spirit of both men and women."

"An affluent gray-haired gentleman summed it up succinctly at the opening of the Men's Club," confided Marion. "In my all-time favorite compliment, he said, 'You are a thoroughbred amongst a group of ponies.' It was great therapy." I wonder if this "affluent gray-haired gentleman" ever made comments like that to his wife. It may have been great therapy for Marion, but when the "affluent gray-haired gentleman" went home, he would have to account for his time. Marion mistook manipulation for a loving compliment.

In moments of lust and deception many men will say things to dancers that they don't say to their wives. Hearing

"I love you" is not uncommon for dancers. "This sort of talk is more obscene to me than sexual talk," said Heidi. "He probably has a wife who would give anything to hear those words."[9] Heidi was savvy enough to see through the lie.

The club owners, the very people who appear to care for them the most, also deceive dancers. It is a relationship based on what the dancer can do for the owner. It is all about taking — while pretending to care.

If the women try to get out of the business, management discourages them. "They are told that no one will ever hire a stripper," said Carolyn McKenzie. "It is a constant barrage that beats them down." These are words spoken by the same people who fed the dancer's self-esteem in an effort to get them to strip in the beginning. First they are deceived into dancing, then they are deceived into staying.

"I felt so empty inside that I wanted to kill myself," said Kimberly, who eventually found faith in God. "It's a cruel business. It's all about self. It's all about using people. There's no love in it. It's like selling your soul. And it's humiliating. It starts with your search for money, and later you end up seeking only approval from men. Then that's not enough, and you need (plastic) surgery and new cars and fancy clothes. All this selling something you should keep for your husband."[10]

Of course, many women in the sex industry are trapped in a deceptive web. The comment that has grieved me most of all was from the mouth of Heather Kozar, the 1999 Playboy Playmate of the Year. In June 1999 she boasted on the "Howard Stern Show," "I'm a born-again Christian who has set her own rules."

I had trouble understanding how she could say something so incredible. I found my answer on her web page where she proudly proclaimed; "Playboy has been my number one priority." That was obvious. It was also obvious that the one who "prowls like a roaring lion seeking someone to devour" has deceived her.

DECEIVING THE CHILDREN

Many dancers are mothers trying to make ends meet. As their children grow, they must also be a part of the deception. "I thought about what my son would say at Career Day," said Susan. "Would he tell them that his mommy takes off her clothes for men?" How long could Susan hide her occupation from her son? One day she would be found out and the deception would finally come to an end.

DECEIVING THE GOVERNMENT

It should come as no surprise that much of the income dancers make is left unreported. Many dancers fail to file income taxes since they receive their money in tips. "Twenty percent of the girls pay taxes like they're suppose to," said Diane, a 25-year-old stripper. "The others don't pay, or if they do, they'll claim $30,000 when they really made $100,000."[11]

DECEIVING OUR NEIGHBORHOODS

Many clubs are a public health problem. "Normal citizens don't have a clue what goes on in these clubs," said Carolyn McKenzie. She said some dancers in Memphis wash themselves with warm water and lemon juice during the evening thinking it will kill germs. Amazingly enough, these clubs are moving closer and closer to our neighborhoods. I honestly think that if the public knew the dangers of these clubs there would be a public outcry to shut them down. It won't happen until we stop buying into the deception.

Writer George Will said, "One doesn't need a moral micrometer to gauge the fact that the sex industry turned Times Square into a slum." The facts seem to support his statement. Land-use studies have shown that communities surrounding a sexually oriented business have prostitution, increased sexual assaults, and increased criminal activity.[12]

In Tucson, Arizona, an investigation was conducted

and police officers found a wide variety of illegal sexual conduct at every sexually oriented business investigated. Almost every business had employees arrested for prostitution or obscene sex shows. Many underage dancers were found, with the youngest being a 15-year-old girl.[13]

The city of Los Angeles compared its statistics on crime in areas with sexually oriented businesses with the statistics of a survey conducted in 1969. The results were shocking. Pandering is up 340 percent, murder 42 percent, aggravated assault 45.2 percent, robbery 52.6 percent, and purse snatching 17 percent.[14]

Another study conducted on sexually oriented business growth concluded, "The best judgment available indicates overwhelmingly that adult entertainment businesses — even a relatively passive adult bookstore — have a serious negative effect on their immediate environs."[15]

"The mere presence of sexually oriented businesses negatively influences the public's perception of the neighborhood in which they are located," said Mary Poss, mayor pro tem for the city of Dallas. "SOBs can create 'dead zones' in commercial areas because shoppers do not want to be associated with these businesses or have their children exposed to the surroundings. The public perception is that it is a place to be avoided by families."[16]

Poss' belief is supported by an appraiser questionnaire distributed to 400 real estate professionals. Over 87 percent of the respondents felt sexually oriented businesses would decrease the market value of their business property.[17]

A police department analysis in Dallas showed 911 calls were taken from seven sexually oriented business in one area on an average of at least one per day per club over a four-year period. During that period, the analysis indicated 396 arrests for sex crimes.[18]

The worst deception of all may be that we feel this is not our problem. Marriages are being destroyed, women are being kept in bondage and men are lost in a world of lust, and yet citizens across the country don't see the problem.

   The filth of sexually oriented businesses can be found inside the club and out . . . and marriages are being destroyed in the wake. The only winners are the managers of the clubs and their victory is short-lived. One day in the not so distant future they will have to give an account to a holy and righteous God. The deception will finally end.

1 "Rags and Riches," *Fort Lauderdale Sun-Sentinel*, November 11, 1997.
2 Ibid.
3 Heidi Mattson, *Ivy League Stripper* (New York: Arcade Pub., 1995), p. 120.
4 "Adult Industry Spins a Web of Profit," *Fort Lauderdale Sun-Sentinel*, November 13, 1997.
5 Sylvia Plachy and James Ridgeway, *Red Light — Inside the Sex Industry* (New York: Powerhouse Books, 1996), p. 183.
6 "Rags and Riches," *Fort Lauderdale Sun-Sentinel*.
7 Ibid.
8 Ibid.
9 Mattson, *Ivy League Stripper*, p. 11.
10 "On the Dark Side: The Hidden Costs," *Fort Lauderdale Sun-Sentinel*, November 14, 1997.
11 "Rags and Riches," *Fort Lauderdale Sun-Sentinel*.
12 "Sexually Oriented Business," National Coalition for the Protection of Children and Families.
13 Ibid.
14 "Facts about Pornography," American Family Association.
15 "Sexually Oriented Businesses," National Coalition for the Protection of Children and Families.
16 Letter from Mary Poss, June 20, 1997.
17 "Facts about Pornography," American Family Association.
18 Letter from Mary Poss, June 20, 1997.

11

Her Name Is Not Barbie

> Do you not know that your bodies are members of Christ? Shall I then take away the members of Christ and make them members of a harlot? May it never be! (1 Cor. 6:15).

I ONCE HEARD THAT A GROWN WOMAN with a figure proportioned to that of a Barbie doll would have trouble walking upright. Unfortunately, today I think men are looking for Barbie. Some men gaze at *Sports Illustrated*'s swimsuit issue, others are fascinated with Victoria's Secret catalogs. A model wearing nothing or almost nothing is sure to get the attention of a man.

The sex industry wants to profit from men's fascination with the female body. The last area of adult entertainment we'll look at is nude modeling, which often leads to prostitution. Nude modeling studios flourish in many cities across America. We'll look at three types of "agencies."

Personal modeling
Professional modeling studios
Streetwalkers

PERSONAL MODELING

Personal modeling is big business according to Detective Paul Ronyak from the Dallas Police Department's vice section. Several years ago adult newspapers in Dallas had 2 pages of women who would "model" for men. Today the same newspapers carry 14 pages of such ads. The ads contain a picture of a beautiful topless woman with her name and phone number. Unless the picture says "actual photo," you are not getting the same woman, although she'll go by the same name. Uh oh . . . the deception has already begun.

Personal models cost $100–$200 an hour, depending on what they let men do. Although some from this category are involved in prostitution, most are not. I called one inquiring about prices, and without my asking, she said she did not offer "full service." I wondered if I had called a gas station by mistake.

Models offer in-call and out-call services. In-call means the man comes to her place, usually an apartment or hotel room. Out-call offers men the wonderful opportunity to have a model show up on your doorstep. Not only will she show up, but also a male driver will wait patiently outside for her to return to the car. If you buy an hour, their bodyguard knocks on your door if you keep her longer.

Personal models may be college students or housewives looking for extra money. I asked the one I called if she was the girl in the picture. I knew she wasn't, but her answer surprised me. "No," she said smoothly, "I'm prettier." I was convinced she had used that line in the past to begin a web of deception. Detective Ronyak told me that not only is the model I talked to not the one in the picture, she is not even the one I would see if I engaged her services. Many modeling agencies have answering services to field calls so the phone experts can "sell" the customers before models show up.

Before I ended my phone conversation with the "model," I told her what she was doing was destroying families. She defended herself by saying all she did was nude modeling. "I know," I replied. "And that's destroying families." After ten seconds of silence, she hung up without saying another word.

When I called another model she told me to go a restaurant at a designated time and call her again. When I made the second call, she would give instructions on where to go next. The purpose of the second call is to help weed out the crank callers. I had no need to find out what was next, so I never made the second call.

Some men have been ripped off during this experience. "Mickey Fin girls put drugs in the drinks and when the man wakes up, everything is gone," said Detective Ronyak. While that normally does not happen, it is another reminder of how the models will do whatever it takes to get what they want. Of course, the same is true of the men. Women are using men and men are using women. And everyone loses.

A model named Holly who is still in the business told me that many men show up and say, "I've never done this before." She explained that some men would circulate to avoid having the appearance of being a regular customer. Other men like being regular customers. One of Holly's regular customers is an 86-year-old man who has a terrible odor and declines Holly's invitation to take a bath. Most of the clients Holly serves are married men.

While the deception is obvious, most of these women hate what they are doing. I met with a woman named Megan who decided to leave the "modeling" industry. "I hate not being able to tell my children what I do," Meagan claimed. "I also don't like the risk factor since I am coming in contact with someone's fluid."

Megan had been in the sex industry for ten years so I asked her how many of the women she had met were sexually abused as children. "Oh, all of them," she replied. I had figured the answer was high, but it was as if I had asked a dumb question. Why else would a woman try to make a living selling her body unless she had a tragic past?

Before Megan and I spoke, one of her "clients" called her to set another appointment, she told him that she wasn't doing it anymore. She had recommitted her life to Christ and was involved in a support group with other women who had left the industry.

When her client heard why she was leaving and what she was involved in, he said, "I wish there was something like that for me." Megan said to me, "Henry, I hope you don't mind, but I gave him your name and phone number." Mind? I was thrilled.

PROFESSIONAL MODELING STUDIOS

Modeling studios offer men seeking sexual activity privacy and secrecy as they indulge their lust. Telephones at these studios are usually answered with a simple "hello." The buildings don't have windows. You can't walk in the front door without knocking or ringing a bell first. They are dimly lit. Surely no one will ever find out! Men deceive themselves into believing they are being "discreet," but one day the Lord will bring light to the things hidden in darkness (1 Cor. 4:5). Sin cannot be hidden forever. One day the discreetness comes to an end.

Many studios are open 24 hours, round the clock. The woman behind the counter may be dressed in underwear or other revealing attire. Some studios have a row of women standing by waiting for your selection. Each is dressed in sexy lingerie and greets customers with an inviting smile. All men have to do is pay and choose.

"We would be watching television or just talking when the doorbell rang," said Jill, who worked with her friend Sara, "modeling" lingerie in South Carolina. "As soon as the bell rang we had to stand up and strike a pose. I felt like I was on the auction block. It was very degrading and I had mixed emotions. I hoped he'd choose me since I needed the money but there was also a sense of relief because I didn't want to do it. It's not modeling. It's blatant prostitution."

Men rent a small room for $20–$40 for 20 minutes to an hour based on a fee normally posted in the lobby. First-timers may be excited at the low cost, but they are informed that the fee is for the room only. Imagine that. Paying $40 to sit in a room alone for 30 minutes. The cost for company depends on what the customer has in mind. Models may be evasive about the actual cost and simply say, "It depends how much fun you want to have." They are vague to protect the studio from undercover policemen. Once they are in the room with the client, the model is more specific on cost. They net from 10–20 percent of the cut, plus any tips they can get from the man.

Several years ago studios were called tanning salons. Funny thing about adult tanning salons, they didn't have tanning beds. According to Detective Ronyak, the most light you would find was a 100-watt bulb. To be called a tanning salon, laws stated that they had to have tanning equipment so many changed their name to modeling studio.

Many modeling studios, advertised as lingerie or nude modeling, are filled with prostitutes. The more men pay, the more the model will do. Models make money by accommodating desires. When a man enters the dimly lit room, he finds only a chair to sit in. When I spent a day with Dallas vice officers, we visited several modeling studios. The rooms and stained chairs were disgusting.

The model invites her client to make himself comfortable. She may hand him a washcloth or a box of Kleenex. Often she asks him to undress. As she performs, sometimes on a small 2-foot by 4-foot stage near him, the man exposes himself and masturbates, ejaculating into the washcloth or Kleenex.

Most men come in with the expectation of intercourse and it is often delivered. As the model dances, she says, "Would you like me to continue?" As long as the man keeps giving her $20 bills, she keeps going.

"If they don't get what they want," said Jill, "they will leave angry. We are taught to make them pay for each fantasy. It was a cat and mouse game to see who was going to get what they wanted first." As soon as the money is gone, the time is up. Typically a man spends 15 minutes in a room, even though he may have paid for a half-hour. Most men are anxious to leave after they have an orgasm so few complain about the time. If they do complain, they will be reminded that the fee was for "up to" 30 minutes. By playing with words, the model deceives the man.

The women try to build relationships with the men to get them to come back and ask for them again. Sometimes the model will try to set up something on the side to avoid having to pay the studio the room fee.

The job has a horrible impact on the models. "It was my worst experience ever," claimed Jill. "You can't call it entertainment and you can't call it dancing. It's prostitution." Disease is a constant, but unspoken, concern. "We turned a deaf ear and blind eye to disease," said Jill, "but it was very real." The owners tried to make the models believe that the condoms would take care of disease but most of the models knew the truth.

Jill didn't stay long in the business, but her friend Sara kept working as a model. For a lot of the women, modeling is easier than stripping at clubs. When they are not "working" they are sitting around talking or watching television. At the clubs, they hustle constantly which can be exhausting.

"It's easier," admitted Jill, "but it's much more horrific." The experience falls short of my idea of a romantic encounter. I can't imagine a Christian man walking out unashamed.

STREETWALKERS

The women at the bottom of the pile are prostitutes — street walkers. Most are unattractive and wouldn't get a second look by men if they were in any other business. In the sex industry, their "product" sells to sexually addicted men. One vice officer told me men have been arrested who work as doctors, pastors, and many other professional occupations. Only an addict would play the high-risk game of sex with a prostitute for a moment of lust.

Vice officers describe prostitutes as walking diseases. The lust lasts just a moment, but the consequences can last a lifetime. In the wake of their lust, relationships and marriages are destroyed. And for some men, their lust finally ends with their death from disease.

Barbie dolls are not reality and neither are the models in adult entertainment. Many of these women would never get in the door of a professional modeling agency. The best they can do is sell sex to strangers. For the Christian man, the reality of hurting another person is much more obvious. Meagan told me about a time when a man came to her apartment for an appointment and he noticed her Bible on the table. He left immediately. This was probably a Christian man, and the reality of God's word sent him fleeing.

Of all the forms of sexual entertainment I have reviewed, I believe men trapped in relationships with these women are closest to getting caught. They don't get to this point overnight. For most men, sexual encounters with models and prostitutes is years in the making. It won't be long until their sin finds them out. All that will be left are the consequences.

12

The Lust of the Flesh
—— A Day of Vice

Finally, brethren, whatever is true, whatever is honorable, whatever is right, whatever is pure, whatever is lovely, whatever is of good repute, if there is any excellence and if anything worthy of praise, let your mind dwell on these things (Phil. 4:8).

MY DAY STARTED EARLY AS I DROVE down Central Expressway in Dallas. My directions to meet with a sergeant in the vice section were good, but I was not familiar with the downtown area. The office was in a covert location so I had to wander around a bit to find it. Fortunately, I left my home early allowing me to arrive at his office with minutes to spare.

Since I work in a modern corporate environment, the surroundings in the vice section seemed antiquated. Old typewriters and computers sat on desks that looked like they were built in the 1970s. I was directed to the office of a sergeant named David. He was very pleasant and I could tell we were going to hit it off instantly. David is also an ordained Baptist minister. As I had hoped, he was full of information. David introduced me around to the other officers he worked with, many of whom were Christians.

We spent the morning talking about a variety of topics, from church activities to sexually oriented businesses. I felt good about our conversation because he confirmed for me much of what I had written about the destructive world of adult entertainment.

He told me about Texas laws which require sexually oriented businesses to be 1,000 feet from a residence, church, hospital, historic district, park, school, or another sexually oriented business. I learned about the difference between a Class A dance hall license and a sexually oriented business license. All adult establishments are required to have one or the other. Dance hall licenses mean it is illegal for dancers to dance topless, though clubs get around that by having dancers wear flesh colored pasties. It seemed like a game the adult industry played with the police.

David pulled out a stack of mug shots of prostitutes taken after they had been arrested. As I looked at the pictures, I saw hopelessness in their eyes. Many of the women were crying when the picture was taken. I couldn't imagine a woman feeling worse than getting arrested for selling her body to strangers.

I asked David about adult businesses and was surprised to learn that they don't want an adversarial relationship with the police. Clubs don't need enemies on the police force, so some do their best to stay within legal boundaries. Other clubs test the laws to see what they can get away with.

After lunch with the sergeant, his captain, and a friend from Internal Affairs, David and I hit the streets. Before we left I had to sign a waiver of liability saying that I released the city of Dallas and the police department from any liability resulting from our time together.

Our first stop was one of the top clubs in Dallas. David wanted to show me the full spectrum of what Dallas offers so we started on the high end. As we walked towards the door, I felt like I was in a wealthy neighborhood. The beautiful brick building and well-kept landscape could have been on a convention center postcard showing off our city. As we entered, David immediately identified himself and asked for the manager so we could check their license to make sure it was current. What surprised me was how we were received. A nice greeting and handshake from the club manager made me feel more like a relative than a guy tagging along with a vice officer.

After he verified that the license was current, David told the manager that we would go inside and look around. When we opened the doors to the club I received my second surprise. From my visits to strip clubs 20 years ago, I remembered nasty, smoke-filled rooms that reeked of stale cigarette smoke and alcohol. This club smelled like my smoke-free office. David explained that the club had installed a purifier to get rid of the smell. I also noticed how underdressed David and I were compared to the other men. We wore golf shirts and blue jeans and were by far the most casually dressed men in the dimly lit club.

When we sat down, a waitress was at our table within seconds. She had a confused look on her face when David declined a drink, saying, "No thanks, we won't be here long." It was obvious that the word had not gotten around that he was a police officer. To the waitress I suppose his answer sounded more like, "No thanks, we're just looking."

The dancers were my third surprise. The best word I can come up with to describe them is "stunning." They looked like super models. David explained that some of the dancers live in other cities and fly into Dallas to dance on weekends, making over $1,000 a night.

A beautiful dancer was performing a lap dance for a

man in his late fifties or early sixties. The law in Dallas states that dancers can't touch customers, but if these two were not touching I'm sure all you could get between them was a strand of hair. As I looked at the man and the smile on his face, I wondered if he had a wife at home or a daughter the same age as the almost-naked woman in front of him.

We left after less than 15 minutes in the club. As we drove away I thought about why women who were so beautiful would do such a thing. The answer is simple. Where else could they get over $1,000 for one day's work? How long would they stay in the business? Over time, their finely chiseled bodies would self-destruct. I am certain that the club owners wouldn't be around to pick up the pieces.

The second club was at the lower end of the spectrum. We opened the first set of double doors and were instantly hit by the smell of stale smoke I remembered from my days at sexually oriented businesses. David asked the woman who was collecting the cover charge if he could see the manager. Once again he gave them his card identifying himself as a police officer.

The manager at this club received us much differently. He was very nervous. His face gave him away almost instantly. He led us to the back of the club as he held David's card. Suddenly, he stopped before going behind the bar where the license was hung and asked for my card, too. I explained that I was not a policeman and said nothing more. He had a puzzled look on his face but didn't dare try to make an issue of the fact that I was a civilian. I felt like he was hiding something, so I knew he would not send me outside to wait for David. We were in control and he knew it.

The license for this club was current so David and I stood and watched what was going on for a few minutes. This club was different. The dancers looked rough and hardened. I didn't see dancers smiling and laughing like I saw at the previous club. The previous dancers had learned the art of an inviting, deceptive smile. The expressions of the dancers told me this was a job, not a joy. They fought to make eye contact with men sitting in the club. I felt pity as I looked around the room. The men looked rough, too. We left the last club underdressed, yet in this club I felt over-dressed wearing my clean golf shirt and jeans.

On our way to the next club I asked David why men would go to this club when the women at the previous club were much more attractive. He said some men prefer the hardened look. A man who desired to try to take a dancer home had a much better chance at this club. David said that some men try to build relationships with the dancers in the hope of sleeping with them. At the nice clubs the dancers give off the impression that they are out of your league.

At the final club we entered we found an expired license. We also observed a woman performing a lap dance and she was all over the man. There was no doubt they were touching, though the man didn't seem to mind. We saw the woman at the counter walk over to the dancer and whisper something in her ear. Within moments the dancer backed a few feet away from the man. It was obvious that she had been told police were in the building.

A woman wearing a g-string on the main stage was swinging on a pole. Only one man was watching her per-form. Most of the men just sat at the bar and talked with dancers sitting next to them. The club was lifeless and depressing. I was anxious to leave.

Our last stop was to an adult bookstore where we went without David identifying himself as a policeman. At the clubs, I noticed men sitting together. It appears men like to go to the clubs in groups. Adult bookstores are different. Men go to these places alone. We entered and saw rows of illegal hard-core magazines and videos. The customers quietly kept to themselves and didn't make eye contact with anyone else. David and I, however, were looking all around. It seemed to make the manager nervous. We passed by a theater located in the building, but we didn't go in. I didn't need to see what was going on in there — my ears told me all I needed to know.

We walked out a few minutes later and the manager followed us and stood at the door until we drove away. I asked David why the manager was so concerned. He informed me that the manager may have thought one of three things: we were gay, we were robbers casing the place, or we were policemen. The message was clear to both of us — we were not welcome.

That night I told my wife, Kathy, about my day. She was concerned for me and asked if being in sexually oriented businesses and seeing topless women had an effect on me. I told her honestly that while I was in the clubs I didn't have a battle with lust. I felt more like a reporter than a patron. The next week, though, was difficult for me. The memory of the day was replayed in my mind time and time again. I tried to take thoughts captive for Christ. While I found the experience to be helpful in my writing, I was mentally paying for the experience.

After studying this issue for four years, I thought that as I entered the clubs I would see the obvious signs of pain and abuse that I had seen in so many women during my months of interviews. I didn't get to see the signs like I imagined. The difference was that during my visit, I saw the wrong side of the mask. For the most part I saw what they wanted me to see, not the pain behind the mask that each dancer wore. The dancers didn't allow themselves to be vulnerable like the women I had interviewed. They didn't tell me about their troubled past. I didn't see deception; I saw delight.

I was scared because I knew the battle was real. Without my relationship with Christ, any one of those men in the clubs could have been me. I knew I never wanted to enter another club again.

God protected me with David, a vice officer and ordained Baptist minister. I didn't stare in the clubs because

I was with David and we had both given our lives to Christ. Had my escort been a vice officer who was *not* a believer, I don't know how I would have responded. I don't want to know. It was also important to remember as I entered the clubs that I had a wife at home who loved me. And I loved her.

I realized, however, that it is vital for me to be sensitive to God's leading as I get involved in the fight against pornography and adult entertainment. The moment I get involved without Him, I'm in trouble. My visit reminded me about the strength of the temptation. It's powerful. Yet no matter how great the temptation, our God is so much greater.

13

The Peril of Pornography

> The one who commits adultery with a woman
> is lacking sense; he who would destroy himself
> does it (Prov. 6:32).

PORNOGRAPHY AND ADULT ENTERTAINMENT have a cost . . . and it's steep. Men can deceive themselves and think that the only cost is what they pay for the video, magazine, or phone call. Sadly, those men have not even begun to count the cost.

When one Christian man was caught by his wife viewing pornography, he told her, "Variety is the spice of life!" He had no idea of the cost until after his divorce. The peril of pornography is that it leads to destruction. Notice that I did not say "may lead to destruction." Destruction is a step which pornography and adult entertainment cannot miss. Its aim is accurate and its target is precise.

Let's take a moment and count the cost. When you face temptation in the days to come, this chapter will be worth a quick review. Before you buy a new car, you always count the cost. No one would walk into a car dealer and say, "Oh no, I don't need to know how much it costs. Just fill in the amount on my check." Instead, we kick the tires, sit behind the wheel, go for a test drive, and ask a million questions before we make the purchase. We also count the cost before carefully writing the check.

We should treat sexual temptation the same way. Before you give in, count the cost — the peril of pornography. When you finish, ask yourself if it is a price worth paying.

We will find the following in our sexual temptation checkout line.

1. *Pornography distorts reality.* Don't think for a minute that the women are who they appear to be. Nothing could be further from the truth. At one time pornographers airbrushed the nude women in magazines, but now with computer technology, they can make them drop-down-dead gorgeous with computer enhancement techniques. Pornography is built on deception, and it begins by turning the women into something they are not.

As we saw in previous chapters, women in adult entertainment work hard to have men think that they love sex and are attracted to men. That's not reality either. Without exception, every woman I interviewed who had come out of the adult entertainment business said they hated the men. We see the smile that they want us to see, but they would never allow us to see the pain behind their eyes, which runs deep. The money is in deception, not in honesty.

Men who battle with pornography are not engaged in a world of reality. They are lost in a world of fantasy, which is doing great harm. Is a fantasy world dangerous? I believe it is. As we have seen earlier, fantasy is an addiction that grows and grows. It needs an ever-increasing dose or frequency to give you the pleasure you seek. That, of course, is not the worst of it. Men living in a world of fantasy often act out their fantasies.

The problems caused in marriages are extensive. Real women cannot possibly have the same sexual appetite women in adult entertainment appear to have. They lead us to believe that a woman who enjoys sex around the clock is a possibility. Pornography isn't real — it's deceptive. It has nothing to do with love and everything to do with lust, which grieves the heart of God.

2. *Pornography destroys a wife's self-esteem.* Don't miss this one. I remember driving to my college reunion. My wife told me she wanted me to be proud of her when she met my classmates. Of course I told her I already was, but the comment spoke volumes to me. My opinion of my wife mattered to her greatly. She wanted to look her best . . . for me. She wanted me to be proud of her.

Imagine the pain I could cause by pulling out a *Playboy* magazine and saying, "Sweetie, why don't you look like Miss April?" That's exactly what you do when your wife finds out that you are involved in pornography. You're telling her that you prefer someone else and that she does not quite measure up. Can you think of a quicker way to destroy your wife's self-esteem? Guys, lust is a destructive weapon aimed at the heart of the woman who stood next to you the day you said "I do."

In her book *"An Affair of the Mind,"* Laurie Hall wrote, "Jack (her husband) also expressed irritation when I was uncomfortable with some of the sexual practices he'd seen in pornographic magazines. In the end he lost all interest in me as a sexual partner. This had a devastating impact on my view of my worth as a woman. It created such despair in me that I began to let my appearance go. At last, I looked the way his rejection made me feel — totally unlovely."[1]

I saw the destruction firsthand when I met with a woman named Jessica who weighed 350 pounds. "My husband makes me feel so ugly," she wept bitterly as we spoke on the phone. When I met with her husband the next week he confided that at times he wished his wife was dead. It was obvious he now cared little for his wife's self-esteem.

3. *Pornography never satisfies and always leaves you*

wanting more. Why should this be surprising? It has to leave you wanting more or the industry would die. Could you imagine a man hitting an adult site on the Internet and saying, "Wow, this was great, but I'll never do it again. I've been satisfied." What pornography needs to survive is repeat customers. Some men find a temporary satisfaction, but they know it will not last. The temptation hits again later with greater force. I remember once seeing a commercial about a product that said "satisfaction guaranteed." You won't find that with pornography. It will leave you wanting more because pornography is a pseudo-relationship and it is empty. God designed our needs to be fulfilled through real relationships. We need to invest our energy in our God-given relationships, not the relationships built on deception. We can't feed both.

> Two natures beat within my breast,
> The one is foul, the other is blest.
> The one I love, the other I hate,
> The one I feed will dominate.[2]

I met with a seminary student who told me he was struggling with temptation. He bought an adult video and watched half of it before he was overcome with guilt. He stomped on the video and destroyed it. It didn't satisfy and left him unfulfilled.

C.S. Lewis said, ". . . when we say of a lustful man prowling the streets that he wants a woman. Strictly speaking, a woman is just what he does not want. He wants a pleasure for which a woman happens to be the necessary piece of apparatus. How much he cares about the woman as such may be gauged by his attitude to her five minutes after fruition. One does not keep the carton after one has smoked the cigarettes."[3]

Pornography purchased by Christian men is often destroyed within 24 hours after it has been viewed. Christian men don't keep a library of adult videos and magazines. They are purchased to fulfill a moment of lust and then destroyed. Not only is pornography shameful for the Christian man, but it fails to satisfy and always leaves you wanting more.

AN INMATE NAMED CALVIN

I received a letter from an inmate in Atlanta named Calvin who is in prison as a sex offender. He wrote, "I used to live a life filled with the vileness of pornography. Though I asked many women out on dates, almost all refused me. So, in their place I used an 8x10-inch stand-in. My frequent viewing of such material soon lead to addiction. I started to frequent 24-hour bookstores and topless bars. I also called phone sex lines and viewed X-rated videotapes often. It got to the point where I was spending $50 a week just on magazines. *But, eventually even this was not enough to quench my sexual cravings.* (italics mine) I decided that if women would keep on refusing me I would put them in a position where they could not say no.

"I started flashing women to fill my new lustful desires. I exposed myself to over 20 women before I was caught and put in the county jail. I went to trial and pleaded guilty and was returned to the streets with probation. But now, since I was a known flasher I needed to find a new sexual high — something more secret and not so public. I started breaking into apartments looking for a woman to rape...." Calvin will tell you loud and clear, pornography does not satisfy.

4. *Pornography devalues sex.* Pornography provides a one-sided relationship for that God-given energy that's planted in us to move us toward relationships with our spouse. Sexual release through pornography separates us from our spouse. Relationships take more time, more energy, more commitment of our whole selves. It also requires more vulnerability and trust. The women of pornography and adult entertainment are people we don't even know. It's

a relationship built solely on lust. God's design is one man, one woman, becoming one flesh and living a life in obedience to Him. This relationship is built on love. Sex outside this God-given relationship has no value.

I read about a phone sex operator who wanted to meet a certain man who had been calling. When they finally met, she couldn't stand him. You see, the value of their relationship was built on deception. Deception never has had value. Deception simply destroys.

5. *Pornography creates isolation.* The Christian feels alone while he is engaging in pornography. It's a natural response for most men. "While there is an erotic excitement involved in the decision to attend and in the experience itself," said Scott, a man who knows the struggle of temptation, "this is mixed with considerable amounts of fear and embarrassment. From the instant my car is carrying me toward pornography, I feel painfully visible, as if everyone who sees me knows from my expression, my body language, whatever, precisely where I'm going. The walk from the car to the door — and later, from the door to the car — is especially difficult: will someone drive by and see me?"[4]

We want to be alone to enjoy our "erotic excitement" — alone with a magazine, video, or a computer screen. Alone in an adult arcade or strip club. Alone with our lust. Anything else would be shameful. We pull away from our family and we pull away from God. And we're alone.

6. *Pornography facilitates child molestation.* The facts speak for themselves. An incredible 87 percent of convicted molesters of girls, and 77 percent of convicted molesters of boys, admit to the use of pornography, most often in the commission of their crimes.[5]

"The common thread among all these victims of sexual abuse is pornography," said Lee Shipway, a licensed psychotherapist. "Almost every single one of the children that I have seen, their perpetrators first started out by using pornography as a way to try to meet that emptiness inside their souls. Often times the victims that I work with say, 'I thought everybody's Dad did that to them.' "[6]

Pornography, it seems, is instruction material for child molesters. You're probably not a child molester, but when you purchase pornography, you feed the industry and help keep it alive for child molesters. That price tag alone should drive the Christian user of pornography to his knees.

7. *Pornography is expensive.* I talked to or read about many men with incredible debt resulting from an addiction to pornography and adult entertainment. It's not cheap. A single magazine may cost $10. A phone call to a phone sex operator can ring up costly charges before ever seeing the phone bill. The Internet eventually leads to the use of your credit card. It's addictive and costly . . . and the more it costs, the greater the chance you'll be found out. Many men are caught when their wives see the phone bill or the credit card statement. It's an addiction that needs to be fed, and it enjoys feasting on the bills and cards found in your wallet.

8. *Pornography shapes attitudes and behaviors.* Check with your local prison and ask how pornography shapes the attitudes and behaviors of rapists. It certainly did for "Chuck" who was divorced from his wife after catching her in bed with his cousin: "I went to a porno bookstore, put a quarter in a slot, and saw this porn movie. It was just a guy coming up from behind a girl and attacking her and raping her. That's when I started having rape fantasies. When I saw that movie, it was like somebody lit a fuse from my childhood on up. When that fuse got to the porn movie, I exploded. I just went for it, went out and raped. It was like a little voice saying, 'It's all right, it's all right, go ahead and rape and get your revenge; you'll never get caught. Go out and rip off some girls. It's all right, they even make movies of it.'"

No, most men who look at pornography don't turn into rapists, but it still shapes their attitudes. It shapes how we view women, sex, and certainly how we view sin. In Tom Eisenman's book *Temptations Men Face*, he told of a

Christian leader who viewed pornography and adult entertainment as a reward for "good work done on writing next Sunday's sermon."[7] Make no mistake about it, pornography has tremendous power.

9. *Pornography feeds organized crime.* You may know nothing of organized crime, but it is fed in part by pornography. According to *U.S. News & World Report*, the third-highest form of revenue for organized crime is the sale and distribution of pornography.[8]

"There is a definite casual relationship between pornography and crime," said Shyla Welch, of Enough is Enough. "In the last 30 years since *Playboy* was introduced, sexual violence against women in this country has increased 500 percent."[9]

10. *Pornography kills careers.* Few white-collar workers can survive in the workplace without computers. Most businesses today and even more in the future will provide Internet access for employees. It's a powerful tool in the hand of corporate America, but it is a destructive tool in the hand of a man addicted to pornography and adult entertainment.

In May 1999, Ronald F. Thiemann, Harvard's Divinity School's dean was forced to resign for "conduct unbecoming a dean" after pornographic images were found on his computer. Oh yes, pornography kills careers.

One man I interviewed said he has days where he may spend four hours in porn sites on the Internet. As you read in the chapter on the Internet, men are getting caught in corporate America, and they are losing their jobs. It's hard to keep the addiction locked in the closet at home.

11. *Pornography addiction can be passed to the next generation.* This thought alone should stop the Christian man dead in his tracks. Or maybe you don't think that's possible. Former *Playboy* Bunny Brenda McKillop testified before the Attorney General's Commission on Pornography, and here's what she said:

My first association with *Playboy* began in childhood when I found *Playboy* as well as other pornographic magazines hidden around the house. I have since discovered that a great deal of pornography ends up in the hands of children. This gave me a distorted image of sexuality. . . . I believe that the *Playboy* philosophy of pleasure-seeking lust influenced my father to make passes at other women and to ask a neighbor to swap wives. I believe my mother's battle with obesity caused her to feel jealous of the playgirls and jealous of her own daughter's body. I never questioned the morality of becoming a *Playboy* bunny because the magazine was accepted into the house.[10]

Did you catch that? Her father put her view of pornography in motion because of his addiction. The same holds true for sons. "I remember when my father and I had our 'father and son' chat," said Michael. "All my Dad did was hold open a *Playboy* centerfold and say, 'I thought you might like to know what a naked woman looks like.' All I did was glance because I knew I could get a better look later when my Dad left the magazine lying around the house. I know I'm responsible for my own actions, but in a way I'm angry at my Dad for planting seeds for something that would be a lifelong struggle."

Of course, none of this should be a surprise for the Christian man. It's happened before. Read the Book of 1 Kings and underline verses like 1 Kings 15:3, "And he walked in all the sins of his father which he had committed before him." It's a good exercise and I hope each time you read a verse like that it gets your attention. Make no mistake about it, we have the power to pass our addiction on to our children. The question is, do you want to?

Tonight when you head off to bed, take a peek in your son's room, as he lies sleeping. Kneel next to his bed and look closely at his face. Get close enough to hear him breathe. Then ask yourself this question, "Do I want him to receive from me a legacy of lust?"

Picture you and your son in a relay race. Your lap is almost complete and he takes off running with his hand stretched back reaching for your baton. You stretch forward aiming the baton for his open hand. The hand-off is almost complete, but what will you hand him? If you hand him a legacy of lust, then you have indeed made an impact in the next generation.

12. *Pornography destroys a testimony.* How long have you been walking with the Lord? Are you known at work and in your neighborhood as a committed Christian? Your testimony was built and tested over time. You have no greater privilege than to be seen as a follower of Jesus Christ. The impact of your relationship can be used by the Lord to draw others to Him.

The power of pornography, however, destroys the Christian testimony. Neighbors and co-workers will see you differently. They'll pity your wife being married to a porn addict. Worst of all, you'll be viewed as a hypocrite. You talk the talk but don't walk the walk.

Don't believe me? Mention the name of Jim Bakker and Jimmy Swaggart. What comes to mind with those names is not their walk, but their infidelities. A recent example was Atlanta Falcon player Eugene Robinson. He was an outspoken Christian leader on his team, getting ready to play in the Super Bowl against the Denver Broncos, probably the biggest game of his life. He was in Miami with his Christian teammates and family. Early on Saturday morning he received an award for his "high moral character." Later that same day he was arrested for offering an undercover policewoman $40 for oral sex. Guys, I don't know all the details, but I do know that his testimony has been shattered. Guard and cherish your testimony. Don't let it be destroyed by pornography and adult entertainment.

13. *Pornography destroys women in the sex industry.* You got a glimpse of this fact in chapter 4, but I want to make it again here. These women are given a false sense of self-esteem that does not last.

"When my first cover came out, I was at the liquor store where I used to always cash in my welfare checks," said adult magazine model Candye Kane. "There I was on the cover of *Jugs*, looking so pretty. I was so happy to see myself on that cover. I felt famous. The guy at the liquor store even had me autograph his copy and gave me a tab at the store. I thought I had really hit the big time. I grabbed the magazine and raced home to show it to my mother. It was a strange moment when I realized that she wasn't as excited as I was. I mean, I was the first celebrity in our family."[11]

Imagine that — a mother who isn't excited that her daughter is on the cover of a hard-core porn magazine! Isn't it sad that Kane would think that her mother would be thrilled with her "celebrity" status? Kane later performed in other states as a strip club headliner, but when she arrived in Hawaii, she was sent back because she was fatter in real life than she was in her picture. I doubt that gave her self-esteem a boost.

While some women in the adult entertainment industry may think they are celebrities, that is not what pornography is all about. Susan Brownmiller said, "In pornography our bodies are being stripped, exposed, and contorted for the purpose of ridicule to bolster that 'masculine esteem' which gets its kick and sense of power from viewing females as anonymous, panting playthings, adult toys, dehumanized objects to be used, abused, broken, and discarded."[12] There is not a lot of room for self-esteem development in that definition.

"The women that are used for pornography are just a product," said Steve Lane, who left a lucrative career in pornography after he came to Christ. "That's how we looked at them. They are being used, consumed for the greed of others. And so many girls think that they want to be in these magazines. Well, I think that if people could see a picture of a girl before she enters the pornography industry and then see a picture of her six months later, they would swear that she had aged ten years. And it is a very horrible industry — it's not glamorous, it's not attractive. The truth is that pornography will destroy you from the inside out and it will start with your heart and it will work its way through your whole body and it will ruin your whole life."[13]

The sad part is that women come into the sex industry already defeated. According to Morality in Media, 60–80 percent are adult survivors of childhood sexual abuse.[14] With that history, it should not be a surprise that one study found the following to be true of strippers:

> 35% have multiple personality disorder
> 55% have borderline personality disorder
> 60% have major depressive episodes[15]

"These are women who, when they were little girls, would get into their beds each night and roll themselves into a fetal position and every night he would come in and peel her open," said, Mary Anne Layden, director of education in the Department of Psychiatry at the University of Pennsylvania.[16]

As adults, these women now re-enact their childhood trauma by working in the sex industry. They were compromised as children and are now more vulnerable and accessible to being with people who will re-victimize them. They bond to the trauma that they experienced as children.

The sex industry aids them on the path to destruction. Consider the following about women in the sex industry published by Morality in Media:[17]

Marriage & Abuse	Percentage
Marriages that last over three years	25%
Reported physical or verbal abuse on the job	100%

Types of Assault on the Job by
Customers, and Percentage

Hair pulled	27%
Pinched	58%
Slapped	24%
Bitten	36%

For the non-believer, this may not be a problem. Many men don't care about the women anyway. For the Christian man, however, this ought to stop you cold. Another life is being destroyed, just so your lust can be fulfilled.

14. *Pornography grieves the heart of God.* Pornography leads to lust and lust is sin . . . and sin grieves the heart of God. With pornography we do exactly what we're told not to do.

> And do not grieve the Holy Spirit of God, by whom you were sealed for the day of redemption (Eph. 4:30).

15. *Pornography eventually gives Satan a stronghold in your life.* In his book *Personality Traits of the Carnal Mind,* Dr. Ron Miller wrote, "Willfully seeking after pornographic material opens up one's spirit to demonic influence and even control by an unclean spirit."[18] Is it any wonder that we are told to flee immorality?

That's 15 reasons for us as Christian men to flee from the temptation of pornography and adult entertainment. The Christian walk is difficult in these troubled days. We've lost our moral compass with little hope on the horizon for finding it. Unfortunately, it is also getting harder and harder to distinguish the Christians from the non-Christians. Certainly, pornography levels the playing field. We don't want to be identified with Christ as we engage in adult entertainment. Once we get caught, we no longer have to worry about that. We no longer will be by the people who know us best.

Maybe you have been involved in pornography for some time and have not been caught. This is your secret sin that you have hidden well. Your day of exposure is on the horizon.

In Numbers 32:23, it is written, "Behold, you have sinned against the Lord, and be sure your sin will find you out." Adam was the very first to figure that out. When he and Eve sinned in the garden, they tried to hide themselves from the presence of God. After God asked the question, "Where are you?" Adam knew he had been caught. His sin had found him out.

Need more proof? In Ecclesiastes 12:14 it is written, "For God will bring every act to judgement, everything which is hidden, whether it is good or evil." In Luke 12:2, Jesus himself said, "But there is nothing covered up that will not be revealed, and hidden that will not be made known."

Not only will you be found out, but the consequences will be steep. "Then the Lord passed by in front of him and proclaimed, 'The Lord, the Lord God, compassionate and gracious, slow to anger, and abounding in lovingkindness and truth; who keeps lovingkindness for thousands, who forgives iniquity, transgression and sin; yet He will by no means leave the guilty unpunished, visiting the iniquity of fathers on the children and on the grandchildren to the third and fourth generations' " (Exod. 34:6–7).

The verse tells us of God's compassion and lovingkindness, desiring to forgive the iniquity and transgression of His people. The guilty, however, will not be left unpunished. Your iniquity will visit your *children* and *grandchildren*.

The fact that the addiction can be passed from generation to generation is supported by the medical community as well. In Patrick Carnes' book *Out of the Shadows — Understanding Sexual Addiction* he writes, "For the role of the addict, part of the therapy is to discover the role of the previous generation in the addiction. The exhibitionist who learns that his father, two uncles, and two cousins were also exhibitionists becomes keenly aware that the 'sins' of one generation are visited upon the next."[19]

In Revelation, Jesus addressed the unconfessed sin of immorality, which He held against the church at Pergamum. Jesus gave both command and a harsh warning. "Repent therefore; or else I am coming to you quickly, and I will make war against them with the sword of My mouth" (Rev. 2:16). It's time to deal with the temptation and addiction that plagues you. If you are ready, God is waiting.

> For He delivered us from the domain of darkness, and transferred us to the kingdom of His beloved Son, in whom we have redemption, the forgiveness of sins (Col. 1:13–14).

Your choices are clear — disclosure or deception. One choice leads to redemption while the other leads to continued bondage and pain. Do you still honestly believe that you can keep your sin a secret?

No matter how clever you are, no matter what precautions you take, one day your sins will find you out. Then it will be too late to count the cost. Payment will be due.

1 Laurie Hall, *An Affair of the Mind* (Colorado Springs, CO: Focus on the Family Publishing, 1996), p. 76.
2 Jerry and Kirsti Newcombe, *A Way of Escape* (Nashville, TN: Broadman and Holman Publishers, 1999), p. 150.
3 Dr. David Jeremiah, "Lust and Adultery" tape from the series "How to Live According to Jesus," Vol. 1, produced by Turning Point, San Diego, CA.
4 Michael S. Kimmel, *Men Confront Pornography* (New York: Crown Publishers, 1990), p. 35.
5 W. Marshall, report on the use of pornography by sexual offenders, Federal Department of Justice, Ottawa, Canada.
6 Presentation by Lee Shipway, psychotherapist to the Children Service Society of Wausau, Wisconsin.

7 Tom L. Eisenman, *Temptations Men Face* (Downers Grove, IL: InterVarsity, 1990), p. 53.

8 James Lambert, *Porn in America* (Lafayette, LA: Huntington House Publishers, 1997), p. 101.

9 "Porn Proliferation Linked to Crime," *Credo*, November 15, 1997.

10 Judith A. Reisman, *Soft Porn Plays Hardball — Its Tragic Effects on Women, Children, and the Family* (Lafayette, LA: Huntington House Publishers, 1991), p. 163.

11 Wendy Chapkis, *Live Sex Acts — Women Performing Erotic Labor* (New York: Routledge, 1997), p. 107.

12 Diana E.H. Russell, *Against Pornography — The Evidence of Harm* (Berkeley, CA: Russell Publications, 1993), p. 7.

13 "Free at Last!" *American Family Association Journal*, March 1999, p. 21.

14 Mary Anne Layden, "If Pornography Made Us Healthy, We Would Be Healthy by Now," *Morality in Media*, May/June 1999, p. 4.

15 Ibid.

16 Ibid.

17 Ibid.

18 Hall, *An Affair of the Mind*, p. 121.

19 Patrick Carnes, Ph.D., *Out of the Shadows — Understanding Sexual Addiction* (Center City, MN: Hazelden Publishing Group, 1992), p. xxii.

14

Triumph over Temptation

> But I say to you, that everyone who looks on
> a woman to lust for her has committed adultery
> with her already in his heart (Matt. 5:28).

YOU MADE IT. WE'VE SEEN THE PROBLEM and now it's time to talk about solutions that can help you find victory over temptation. Like the keys on your key chain, they won't do a bit of good unless you use them. Not only do they work today, they have worked throughout history.

Earlier we looked at King David as he failed with Bathsheba. Well, we also have a model for victory. His name is Joseph.

We need to hear the story of Joseph today. Our culture tells us that we are incapable of resisting temptation's call. Lust is ever present. Everyone is doing it. Purity is passé.

Joseph lived in a corrupt culture and yet he stood faithful and true. In Genesis 37 and 39 we read that he was sold into slavery by his brothers and eventually ended up in the home of Potiphar, the captain of the bodyguard under Pharaoh. God caused everything to prosper under Joseph.

He found Potiphar's favor and was made overseer in his house. Joseph was in charge of everything.

You need to know something else about Joseph. He was "handsome in form and appearance." He was the GQ guy of his day. Not only was Potiphar impressed with Joseph, so was Potiphar's wife.

> And it came about after these events that his master's wife looked with desire at Joseph, and she said, "Lie with me" (Gen. 39:7).

Guys, Joseph has a problem. Here was a young good-looking guy who spent his days in slavery. Since Potiphar was an Egyptian officer under Pharaoh himself, I'll assume his wife was beautiful. This must have been quite a temptation for Joseph. What made it even harder was that Potiphar's wife didn't know how to take "no" for an answer.

> And it came about as she spoke to Joseph day after day, that he did not listen to her to lie beside her, or be with her (Gen. 39:10).

Did you notice that? She spoke to Joseph *day after day*. It was a temptation that certainly would have worn down many men. His resistance could have been worn down by her persistence. Not only would resisting temptation be difficult, but Joseph had reasons why it made sense to give in!

Reason #1. Who would have caught them? Certainly Joseph would not have told anyone. His life would have been cut short if he was found out. How about Potiphar's wife? Not a chance. She had too much to lose. How would you react to sexual temptation if you knew for certain that no one would find out?

Reason #2. Joseph wanted to return to his father, Jacob. Slavery was not the occupation he had chosen for his life. He was sold into slavery against his will. Joseph wanted to go home. Who would be a greater ally to help plead his case than the wife of his master?

Reason #3. He was a handsome young healthy male and she was a beautiful woman! Who could blame him? Besides, it's not like he asked for it. (Uh oh, I've started rationalizing.)

It doesn't take much of an attorney to plead Joseph's case for giving in.

> But he refused and said to his master's wife, "Behold, with me here, my master does not concern himself with anything in the house, and he has put all that he owns in my charge. There is no one greater in this house than I, and he has withheld nothing from me except you, because you are his wife. How then could I do this great evil, and sin against God?" (Gen. 39:8–9).

I love those first three words: "But he refused." The text does not give us any indication that Joseph had to think about it. Never did he say, "Gee, that's a great offer for a slave like me." He never weighed the pros and cons. He didn't seek advice from a fellow slave. He never formed a committee for brainstorming. He said no. Joseph was prepared for the answer long before the question was ever asked.

It is also interesting to note the loyalty he had for Potiphar and the shock he had at the thought of sinning against God. "How then could I do this great evil. . . ." Wouldn't it be great if we had the same attitude and were shocked at the very thought of sexual sin?

Charles H. Spurgeon once said, "We are too often in haste to sin. Oh that we might be in a greater hurry to obey!" A hurry to obey? That's Joseph!

In his preparedness, Joseph had to do some practical

things to protect himself. So do we. Take a look at verse 10 again. She sought him day after day, but Joseph "did not listen to her to lie beside her, or be with her." He fled!

KEYS TO VICTORY

Key #1 — Flee

> Now flee from youthful lusts, and pursue righteousness, faith, love and peace, with those who call on the Lord from a pure heart (2 Tim. 2:22).

It is interesting to note that in 1 Corinthians 16:13, men are told, "Be on the alert, stand firm in the faith, act like men, be strong." Yet in the area of lust, we are told to flee. Why is that? I know why it is true for me. My weakness is no surprise to Satan. He loves it when I hang around sexual temptation. He knows what it takes to sift me like wheat.

Earlier in his first letter to the church at Corinth, Paul wrote, "Flee immorality. Every other sin that a man commits is outside the body, but the immoral man sins against his own body" (1 Cor. 6:18). Involvement with pornography and adult entertainment is a sin against our own bodies so Paul instructs us to flee. We would be wise to obey!

Puritan writer Benjamin Needler wrote, "We must not part with sin, as with a friend, with a purpose to see it again and to have the same familiarity with it as before, or possibly greater. . . . We must shake our hands of it as Paul did shake the viper off his hand into the fire."[1] True repentance means change, both of your mind *and* your ways.

"Carl" had made tremendous progress in his fight against pornographic addiction. He found himself spiritu-ally strong and able to flee temptation. "Only a few snipers remain," he said. "Once I failed, just a month later when I was walking the streets of San Francisco. I felt myself pulled — it felt exactly like that — into another of the 25-cent peep shows to watch an undulating girl on a revolving table for three minutes. Not ten seconds passed when I felt a sense of horror. My head was pounding. Evil was taking over. I had to get out of there, immediately. I ran, literally ran, as fast as I could out of the North Beach district."[2]

Carl had once felt safe when he had given in to lust. Now he knew he was safe only when he was far from the temptation. Guys, God said it and I believe it — don't gaze, don't gawk, don't give in — flee!

Key #2 — Fellowship

> Iron sharpens iron, so one man sharpens another (Prov. 27:17).

When I was doing my interviews I was given the name of a woman who I thought was a former strip club owner. I called her on the phone and told her what I was doing and asked if I could interview her. She seemed excited to meet with me. I knew she was aware of the inner workings of clubs. It was a great opportunity.

Before the conversation ended, I asked her what club she had managed. I was surprised with her answer, "I didn't 'use to manage' a club, I still manage Sheer D'lite." She further told me that her hours were 11 a.m. to 7 p.m. so she could not meet for lunch. If I wanted to talk with her, I had to come by the club.

"You don't have a problem coming into a topless club do you?" she asked. This was one of those moments where my mouth was moving, but nothing was coming out. After a short pause I said, "Well, ah, sure, I think we can work that out."

When I hung up the phone I felt a bit uneasy. My motive for going in was to get information for my book. After all, I was doing this for the kingdom of God. Surely, He would understand. Yeah, I knew I could just go in and not look around. I would meet with the manager and get all the information I needed. Her interview would be powerful,

I just knew it. In spite of my rationalization, I still felt uneasy.

I went to see my friend, Jim Cote, my predecessor as the chaplain at Interstate Batteries. Originally, I was a trainer by profession, but for the moment, I was a salesman, telling Jim why he had to buy into my idea and support my great opportunity. I'll never forget his words.

"Henry, don't do it." What? Surely he didn't understand what a great opportunity this was. I pitched him again. "Henry, don't do it." I wondered if his needle was stuck because he kept saying the same thing. He never saw the gold mine. All he saw was the gutter. I left his office a bit discouraged and called Dan Panetti from the Dallas Association for Decency. He had given me the woman's name. Surely he would see the value of the interview. No such luck. He wasn't crazy about the idea either.

Later that night I told my wife about the opportunity and she was the most convincing of all. I wasn't going to have this interview. As I thought about it later, I was convinced that without the fellowship of my wife and these godly men, I would have conducted the interview. I was thinking in a cloud. I want to make the right choices, but sometimes I don't. I got lost in the outcome and never saw the treacherous path I was taking to get there.

Jim asked a question in our discussion that hit me hard, "Henry, are you sure God is going in there with you?" I wondered. Was it God saying, "Go," or Satan saying, "Yes, Henry, come"? I needed the counsel of other godly people to help me understand.

The key word is *godly*. I met with Chris, a single man who said he was tempted to have sex. His pastor told him to give into the urge so it would go away. Chris asked me what I thought about the advice. "Chris," I said. "I think your pastor's advice is from the pit of hell. How did he support his recommendation biblically?" I reminded Chris that if he wants the devil to flee, he needs to resist him.

SOMEONE TO TRUST

"Our secrets can keep us in terrible bondage," said Richard. "The only way I can experience the power of God is with other brothers — by confessing, sharing, and opening my wounds. When I don't have to hide those wounds and sins anymore, they lose a lot of their power."[3]

The topic of sexual temptation is extremely difficult for us to talk about, but we must. Find a man who you trust. Someone you can be transparent with. Someone who won't look at you and say, "And you're a Christian?" Someone who will keep your struggles confidential and hold you accountable for good decisions. In our sex-obsessed culture today, what man would say that he does not need accountability? We need to be able to find these men in our church.

A popular television show in the 1980s was "Cheers." Do you remember the theme song? This bar was a place where everyone knew your name. A place where people were glad you came. A place to take a break from all your worries, where your troubles were all the same. Sad to say, but I wish the church was more like that Boston bar.

A MOMENT OF PRIVACY

Comedian Tim Allen tells an interesting story about a time he was in jail for selling drugs. He was placed in a holding cell with ten other men he didn't know. Located in the middle of the cell was a toilet. It was hard not to notice. Though most men are not very modest, going to the bathroom in front of ten strange inmates would have been difficult, to say the least. After surveying the situation, Allen knew that he would not use the toilet.

"Digestion being as it is," confessed Allen, "things must emerge. I ambled tentatively to the can. I turned away and started back to my seat, but knew it was no good. I was committed. I sat down and suddenly all the men began moving toward me. I panicked."

Can you imagine this scenario? It must have been

humiliating to make the decision to use the toilet, but now he has ten men standing around him as he wonders what is going on.

"What they did was form a horseshoe around me with their backs in my direction," said Allen. Why would they do such a thing for someone they didn't even know? "Because they're men, too," said Allen. "It was a big revelation. These aren't just losers like me, but they are men. They do this so you can have some privacy and no one can see in from the outside." [4]

INTO THE LIGHT

Our sexual sin is shameful and very private. We believe that if other men really knew us with all the walls down, that we would be rejected. We need to remember that Satan is the architect of darkness and as I mentioned in the introduction, our healing begins when we bring our sin into the light.

> And this is the message we have heard from Him and announce to you, that God is light, and in Him there is no darkness at all. If we say that we have fellowship with Him and yet walk in the darkness, we lie and do not practice the truth; but if we walk in the light as He himself is in the light, we have fellowship with one another, and the blood of Jesus His Son cleanses us from all sin (1 John 1:5–7).

We need men who will stand by us, who will keep our shame private as we work through our struggle with God's help. These are men we can be honest with as we discuss our victories and defeats. Paul supports the idea of bringing what is in the darkness into the light. In his letter to the church at Ephesus he wrote, "And do not participate in the unfruitful deeds of darkness, but instead even expose them; for it is disgraceful even to speak of the things which are done by them in secret" (Eph. 5:11–12).

John and Paul support the idea of bringing our sin into the light and so does James! "Therefore, confess your sins to one another, and pray for one another, so that you may be healed. The effective prayer of a righteous man can accomplish much" (James 5:16). Healing won't be found in a self-help book or video, but rather in our confession of sins to one another. That's taking what is in darkness and bringing it into the light.

In Proverbs we are told that men who confess their sins will find compassion. "He who conceals his transgressions will not prosper, but he who confesses and forsakes them will find compassion" (Prov. 28:13). Let's face it — there is great power in a godly man confessing his sin.

Dr. Richard Swenson, who wrote the wonderful book *The Overload Syndrome*, told me at a men's conference that confession is therapeutic! Researchers have called it the "disclosure effect." Simply disclosing a problem improves well-being in measurable ways. Imagine that — confessing our sins to one another can be supported biblically *and* medically.

CAN I ASK YOU SOMETHING?

I've got men like that in my life and I thank God for them. Each week we ask each other these questions:

1. Have you prayed daily?
2. Have you read your Bible daily?
3. What victories have you had?
4. Have you exposed yourself to any explicit material this week?
5. What else?
6. Have you lied to me?
7. What can I pray for you this week?

The "what else" question is asked until we say, "that's it." We confess it all and it makes a difference.

Another thing that worked for some of the guys was to keep a record of victories. Find a calendar and each day you avoid pornography, put a "v" on the calendar for that day. Days that are not victorious are left blank. Show the calendar to your accountability partner. Be open to discuss the days where you suffered defeat. Look closely at the reasons why. What were you doing? What were you thinking? What was your state of mind?

CAN GOD FREE ME FROM MY ADDICTION?

Why are relationships so important in our recovery from sexual addiction? Surely an all-powerful God could take this addiction from you. God created the earth, parted the Red Sea, saved Daniel in the lion's den, crumbled the walls of Jericho, and did much, much more. Freeing you from sexual addiction is certainly within His power. So why doesn't He?

In Luke 8, Jesus came to the house of a man named Jairus, whose daughter had just died. Jesus took her by the hand and said, "Child, arise" (Luke 8:54). Her spirit immediately returned and Jesus gave orders to get her something to eat. Jesus brought her back to life, so why didn't He fill her stomach with something wonderful and delicious? Why did He tell the others to get her something to eat? Could it be that God does the *impossible*, but He requires His people to do the *possible?*

We need the fellowship of godly men who will do the possible in our lives. Men who will come alongside us and hold us accountable to being the men God has called us to be. If you don't have such a person in your life, get on your knees and ask God to help you find such a man.

Key #3 — Follow

Fixing our eyes on Jesus, the author and perfecter of faith, who for the joy set before Him endured the cross, despising the shame, and has sat down at the right hand of the throne of God. For consider Him who has endured such hostility by sinners against Himself, so that you may not grow weary and lose heart (Heb. 12:2–3).

Chuck Colson tells the story of Jack Eckerd, the founder of the Eckerd Drug chain. Fascinated by Colson's views, Eckerd invited him to come to Florida to get involved in prison reform. Although Eckerd was not a Christian, Colson's life and testimony impacted him.

As their relationship grew, Eckerd read some material that Colson had given him. One day Colson received a phone call from Eckerd who told him that he believed Jesus was the Son of God. Colson led him to Christ over the phone.

One day Eckerd went into one of his drug stores and saw *Playboy* and *Penthouse* magazines. He later spoke to his president and told him to remove the magazines from the shelves. The president reminded him that the magazines brought in $3 million dollars a year. Eckerd said he didn't care. By one man's decision, *Playboy* and *Penthouse* were removed from 1,700 Eckerd Drugstores across America.

Colson later asked him if he made that decision because of his commitment to Christ. Eckerd said, "Why else would I give away $3 million dollars?" Eckerd said the Lord wouldn't let him off the hook.

The story doesn't end there. Eckerd later wrote other drug chains asking them to do the same. His request fell on deaf ears until they saw how Eckerd's business began to grow. Other chains followed suit. Revco, Dart Drug, and others took the pornographic magazines off their shelves. The chairman of 7-Eleven, who sat on Eckerd's board, took them out of his stores, too. In a period of 12 months, over 11,000 retail outlets in the United States removed *Playboy* and *Penthouse* from their shelves.[5] The courageous decision was not made due to government involvement. It was because one man had decided to follow Jesus.

If you follow Jesus, will He do the same for you? The apostle Paul seems to think so. "For I am confident of this very thing, that He who began a good work in you will perfect it until the day of Christ Jesus" (Phil. 1:6). If you have accepted Jesus Christ as your Lord and Savior, He began a good work in you . . . and He will perfect it!

In the area of sexual temptation, what does it mean to follow Jesus? In his letter to the church in Rome, I think Paul makes that clear. "Therefore do not let sin reign in your mortal body that you should obey its lusts, and do not go on presenting the members of your body to sin as instruments of unrighteousness; but present yourselves to God as those alive from the dead, and your members as instruments of righteousness to God" (Rom. 6:12–13). The best motivator and best strengthener is to focus on our relationship with God . . . and follow.

Key #4 — Feed

> Thy word I have treasured in my heart, that
> I may not sin against Thee (Ps. 119:11).

We cannot fight effectively if we're not feeding on the word of God. When Satan tempted Jesus, He didn't yield — He quoted Scripture! And I love how He quoted it. Look at the first three words of Jesus' response in Luke 4:12 after the third temptation.

"And Jesus answered." Three words packed with plenty of information. Let's take a look at each one.

1. "And" — Jesus resists the temptation as soon as the last word is out of Satan's mouth. On the heals of the temptation is an immediate response. "And Jesus answered." The key word is *immediately*.

2. "Jesus" — The answer did not come from Peter or John. Jesus had to resist the temptation himself. I wish

I could resist temptation for other men, but I can't. Like Jesus, we have to resist it *personally*.

3. "Answered" — Notice that it does not say, "and Jesus debated" or "and Jesus discussed." It says, "and Jesus answered." Be decisive! As we saw with Joseph, the moment of temptation is not the time to weigh the pros and cons. Answer the temptation *immediately, personally* and *decisively*.[6]

In my survey of over 100 Christian men, I asked them to name one thing they do to protect themselves. Only one man said he memorized Scripture. Guys, that's what Jesus did in Luke 4 when He was tempted by Satan. We would be wise to do the same.

We train our children to dial 911 in case of emergencies. Such a call is good advice when men face "sexual" emergencies, too. That's when we need to dial 311 — Job 31:1: "I made a covenant with my eyes not to look lustfully at a girl." Try repeating that to yourself when you pass an attractive woman at the office. I bet you'll look away. Remember that a man well-fed on the Word of God is stronger in the fight!

Key #5 — Faithfully Pray

Now He was telling them a parable to show that at all times they ought to pray and not to lose heart (Luke 18:1).

The word of God is filled with admonitions to pray. Many of us pray after defeat. We need to pray *before* the battle begins. In Charles Stanley's wonderful book *Winning the War Within*, he has a prayer to help him get dressed each morning. No, he doesn't pray as he puts on his clothes, he prays as he puts on the armor of God.

Prayer for Victory

Good morning Lord. Thank you for assuring me of victory today if I will follow Your battle plan. So by faith I claim victory over _____.

To prepare myself for the battle ahead, by faith I put on the belt of truth. The truth about You, Lord — that You are a sovereign God who knows everything about me, both my strengths and my weaknesses. Lord, you know my breaking point and have promised not to allow me to be tempted beyond what I am able to bear. The truth about me, Lord, is that I am a new creature in Christ and have been set free from the power of sin. I am indwelt with the Holy Spirit who will guide me and warn me when danger is near. I am Your child, and nothing can separate me from Your love. The truth is that You have a purpose for me this day — someone to encourage, someone to share with, someone to love.

Next, Lord, I want to, by faith, put on the breastplate of righteousness. Through this I guard my heart and my emotions. I will not allow my heart to attach itself to anything that is impure. I will not allow my emotions to rule in my decisions. I will set them on what is right and good and just. I will live today by what is true, and not by what I feel.

Lord, this morning I put on the sandals of the gospel of peace. I am available to you, Lord. Send me where You will. Guide me to those who need encouragement or physical help of some kind. Use me to solve conflicts wherever they may arise. Make me a calming presence in every circumstance in which You place me. I will not be hurried or rushed, for my schedule is in Your hands. I will not leave a trail of tension and apprehension. I will leave tracks of peace and stability everywhere I go.

I now take up the shield of faith, Lord. My faith is in You and You alone. Apart from you, I can do nothing. With you, I can do all things. No temptation that comes my way can penetrate Your protecting hand. I will not be afraid, for You are going with me throughout this day. When I am tempted, I will claim my victory out loud ahead of time. For You have promised victory to those who walk in obedience to Your word. So by faith I claim victory even now because I know there are fiery darts headed my way even as I pray, Lord. You already know what they are and have already provided the way of escape.

Lord, by faith I am putting on the helmet of salvation. You know how Satan bombards my day and night with evil thoughts, doubt, and fear. I put on this helmet that will protect my mind. I may feel the impact of his attacks, but nothing can penetrate this helmet. I choose to stop every impure and negative thought at the door of my mind. And with the helmet of salvation those thoughts will get no further. I elect to take every thought captive; I will dwell on nothing except what is good and right and pleasing to You.

Last, I take up the sword of the Spirit, which is Your word. Thank You for the precious gift of Your word. It is strong and powerful and able to defeat even the strongest of Satan's onslaughts. Your word says that I am under no obligation to the flesh to obey its lust. Your word says that I am free from the power of sin. Your word says that He that is in me is greater than he that is in the world. So by faith I take up the strong and powerful sword of the Spirit which is able to defend me in time of attack, comfort me in time of sorrow, teach me in time of meditation, and prevail against the power of the enemy on behalf of others who need the truth to set them free.

So, Lord, I go now rejoicing that You have chosen me to represent You to this lost and dying world. May others see Jesus in me, and may Satan and his host shudder as Your power is made manifest in me. In Jesus name I pray. Amen.[7]

One other thing — when you truly confess your sins — even involving pornography and adult entertainment — to God, you are forgiven. God declares that you are.

If we confess our sins, He is faithful and righteous to forgive us our sins and to cleanse us from all unrighteousness (1 John 1:9).

LESSONS FROM AN ELEPHANT AND MEN NAMED PETER AND DAVID

Do you know how elephants are kept in captivity? When they are babies weighing 300–400 pounds, their trainers will put a shackle around their leg and attach it to a stake. Baby elephants try to break free but they cannot escape. When the baby elephants become massive adults, weighing a couple of tons, they are held captive by the same shackle attached to the same stake. How is that possible? There are two reasons. First, elephants really do have a good memory. Second, they are not very bright. Elephants remember that as babies they could not escape, so as adults, they don't even try. They are not chained to a stake . . . they are chained to the *idea* that they cannot get away.

Men, you are not circus elephants. You are children of God. Take God at His word and seek His forgiveness. Otherwise, feelings of guilt will cripple your progress. Jesus

knew guilty and defeated men long before you were born.
Do you remember Peter? Three times he denied Jesus and
was grieved when the cock crowed, just as Jesus had said.

> And the Lord turned and looked at Peter.
> And Peter remembered the word of the Lord, how
> He had told him, "Before a cock crows today, you
> will deny Me three times." And he went out and
> wept bitterly (Luke 22:61–62).

Jesus was not finished with Peter yet. Peter denied
Jesus three times, and in John 21, Jesus asked Peter three
times if he loved Him. With each positive response Peter
gave, Jesus commissioned him to serve. Jesus never gave up
on Peter, nor will He give up on you.

How about another example? Remember King David?
He committed sexual sin and he was forgiven.

> Because David did what was right in the
> sight of the Lord, and had not turned aside from
> anything that He commanded him all the days of
> his life, except in the case of Uriah the Hittite (1
> Kings 15:5).

Do you see that? Another key word . . . *except*. God
viewed his sin as an exception in his life. When others fail
we have a tendency to identify them by their sin. It's who
they are. Not so with God. Our confessed sin is the exception
and He removes it from us.

> As far as the east is from the west, so far has
> He removed our transgressions from us (Ps. 103:12).

Key #6 — Fall in Love

> An excellent wife, who can find? For her
> worth is far above jewels (Prov. 31:10).

If you're married, your responsibility is to be absolutely committed to you wife and to treasure her. It's a wonderful antidote for the poison of pornography. Tell her you love her often and show it daily by your care for her.

What you cherish about her has to be more than skin deep. "But let it be the hidden person of the heart, with the imperishable quality of a gentle and quiet spirit, which is precious in the sight of God" (1 Pet. 3:4). Fall in love with the qualities she has that some computer or video artist can't enhance.

Remember, pornography rips at the heart of a woman. It destroys self-esteem by introducing other partners into the relationship. According to the National Coalition for the Protection of Children and Families, pornography is usually viewed in secret because men expect a negative response from their wife.

And guess what God considers your wife? "Enjoy life with the woman whom you love all the days of your fleeting life which He has given to you under the sun; for this is your *reward* in life" (Eccles. 9:9).

Imagine that! God calls your wife your reward in life. If you are married, God gave you a wonderful wife — now love her like Christ loved the church.

Key #7 – File

> Therefore, since we have so great a cloud of witnesses surrounding us, let us also lay aside every encumbrance, and the sin which so easily entangles us, and let us run with endurance the race that is set before us (Heb. 12:1).

Have you ever lost a battle buying pornography in a convenience store or renting a movie in some "mom and pop" store? Maybe you didn't buy anything. I bet most of us have gone into such a store and just walked by the rack of magazines or videos just to get an eyeful. That image is

THE SILENT WAR

captured in your mind and now you have to deal with it.

Make a mental file of places where you lost or began to lose battles, then stay away from them. These stores are not convenient if they play a role in your sin. Sin is never convenient.

Many married men struggle with lingerie catalogs that are mailed to their homes. Victoria's Secret may be the worst for men fighting sexual temptation. My wife was on their mailing list and the catalogs came on a regular basis. I wrote them a nice yet forceful letter telling them to stop. They began to look a lot like the *Playboy* magazines that I saw when I was a young boy. I didn't want my son looking at one nor would they do me any good either. If you have lingerie catalogs coming into your home, a simple letter will get you off the mailing list. It is well worth the postage.

Key #8 — Foresee

> But put on the Lord Jesus Christ, and make
> no provision for the flesh in regard to its lusts
> (Rom. 13:14).

We're smart guys. We know where pornography is sold. This falls on the heels of Step #7. Not only do we need to remember where we have been, but we also need to foresee places where pornography *might* be sold.

Mark Twain wrote, "It is easier to stay out than to get out." Makes sense, doesn't it? Getting out of an adult bookstore is much harder than staying out. It is important for us to foresee trouble spots.

On my way home from a family outing I went into a store to buy some Gatorade. My family was in the car. I had no reason to believe that the store contained pornography. As I walked to the back I noticed a row of magazines. There must have been at least 15 different pornographic titles and a box full of videos. I left without my Gatorade. I drove to a Mobil station near my home that I knew did not sell pornography. Behind the counter were the husband and wife owners along with their son. I told him how much I appreciated the fact that they did not sell pornography and that they could count on my business in the future. He told me he would never sell that "dirty stuff." Oh yes, he indeed has my business! I've even ordered a Mobil credit card.

If you want to rent a movie, don't go into a "mom and pop" video store. I can almost guarantee that they will sell adult movies in a back room. Adult movies are big money makers in these places.

If you travel, should you be surprised that a hotel offers pornographic movies? Certainly not. What bothers me about hotels is that they are supposed to be taking care of us while we are away from our families. Instead they throw a temptation in our face. When you check into a hotel, right after you ask how much the room is, ask if they have adult movies. If they do, tell the clerk to unplug your television set — *before* you enter. *Before* is the key word. You can even call ahead and have it dismantled before your plane lands.

If the Internet continues to be a trouble spot for you, get it out of your home. Guys, I know that may sound crazy, but the Internet is an easy place to get into trouble. If I go into a convenience store to buy a pornographic magazine, I may run into my pastor or a neighbor. Not so with the Internet. I can send my family to bed and get locked in porn sites for hours. For some men, the temptation is too great. The chapter on the Internet covered some suggestions to follow before you get to this last drastic step.

I met a man named Carl who played a game he called "Internet Baseball." If he went into a porn site, no matter how long, that was strike one. The second time would be strike two. The third time would be strike three. Three strikes and he would cancel his service. Within two weeks, Carl no longer had the Internet at home. It was a brave decision. He may one day bring it back if he thinks he can handle it, but he assured me that the baseball game would be played if he did.

Other men have mouse pads made with photos of their wife and children. It makes it hard to move the mouse over the face of your family as you search for porn sites. Again, it is just another gentle reminder.

How about your telephone? Listen, even if you are not tempted to call a 900 number for phone sex, call your telephone company and cancel 900 numbers anyway. They are a rip off. If you have sons, it is even more important. Kids make 900 calls, too.

Cable is in the same category. When I see folks with satellite dishes, I shudder at what they can bring into their home. At home I have the basic cable package. HBO, Showtime, Cinemax, and the others are kept out of the house. One night my ten-year-old daughter was punching in numbers on the remote control. She came across an adult channel. The screen was blurred with only faint images, but the audio was crystal clear. The moans and groans of two people were alive in my home. I called the cable company and asked them to block that station completely. I was surprised when they told me they couldn't do anything about it.

Very nicely, I replied, "Well, okay, go ahead and cancel my service." All of a sudden it was within their power to block channels. They sent a man out the next day to fix my problem. I had to either call their bluff or cancel my service. I don't want to mess with the temptation.

The point is, if pornography of any kind is accessible, you are just one weak moment away from defeat. Don't walk into minefields!

Key #9 — Fortify

> Finally, brethren, whatever is true, whatever
> is honorable, whatever is right, whatever is pure,
> whatever is lovely, whatever is of good repute, if

there is any excellence and if anything worthy of
praise, let your mind dwell on these things (Phil.
4:8).

It is hard to lust when you fill your mind with wonderful
things. Many men make it fine until their family is asleep.
The battle seems to get more intense after dark. If you're
married, start praying with your wife before bedtime and
then turning in when she does. If you travel, always take a
framed picture of your family with you and put it on your TV
set. And don't forget to call your family each night along
with your accountability partner. These people really care
about you!

You may also want to cover the screen with a towel
from the bathroom. Your picture can hold it in place! Both
are visual reminders of your commitment to stay pure on the
road.

We fortify our position as we discipline our minds and
rely on God's Spirit. Trust God to give you the proper
motivation as you pray, study God's Word, attend church,
and fellowship with other believers.

Key #10 — Focus on the Female

> And the Lord God fashioned into a woman
> the rib which He had taken from the man, and
> brought her to the man (Gen. 2:22).

Stop and pause each time you are tempted, and remember that these women are created in the image of God. They
are someone's daughters. Imagine how you would feel if it
was *your* daughter. Our lust for them keeps them in bondage
and grieves the heart of God, because they are His daughters.

In Luke 7:37–39, what do you think Jesus thought
about when He had a prostitute weeping at his feet and
wiping the tears with her hair? If that isn't bad enough she
kisses His feet and anoints them with perfume. What would

you think about if a prostitute were at *your* feet? Would you be like the Pharisee who saw a sinful woman who sold her body for a living or like Jesus who saw a woman who needed forgiveness? Would your response be lust or love? For Jesus it was love and He showed her compassion. Men, that should be our response today to the women trapped in adult entertainment. See the women as Jesus saw the women and hang those pictures in the hallway of your mind.

Key # 11 — Financial

One man in Dallas was tempted to go into an adult bookstore. He fled from the temptation and sent the money he would have used for an adult video to the Dallas Association for Decency. Check with your local group — they can always use your financial support.

Men who struggle may also want to limit the amount of money that they have in their possession. John told me that he often stopped at adult bookstores on his way to work. I told him to take only enough money each day to buy lunch. If you don't have it, you can't spend it.

THE COST OF SIN WORKSHEET

Well you know the problem and some solutions to victorious living. Are you ready for an exercise? It's easy. All you have to do is finish this sentence: "If I consistently give in to sexual temptation, these are the consequences I may face in the future. . . ."

What you need to do is take the pain of the future and bring it into the present. As you finish the sentence above, think how this sin would affect you, your family, God, your church, etc. Think of as many answers as you can. When you write your list, make it personal. Don't say, "My wife will lose trust in me." Say, "My wife, _____, will lose trust in me."

Pastor Jim Johnson of Fellowship Bible Church in

Longview, Texas, showed me the exercise and I told him I hated writing the names of the people I love the most. As I looked at the list when I was finished, I asked myself this question. "Is there anything on this list that is an acceptable consequence for giving in to sexual temptation?" Of course, the answer was no. I shrunk my list down, laminated it and put it in my Bible. It is worth reading again and again.

IN THE WILDERNESS WITH JESUS AND MOSES

Being a history major I can tell you when the Civil War ended. General Lee surrendered on April 9, 1865. Satan, however, will not surrender. He is a roaring lion seeking someone to devour (1 Pet. 5:8). Someone like you. The good news is that there is hope!

When Jesus was tempted in the wilderness, Satan did not give up easily. What can we learn today from Jesus' confrontation and victory that will help us in our fight? Here are a few lessons that are worth remembering:

1. *Satan is persistent.* Jesus was tempted once? Twice? No — three separate times that are recorded in the text. He will not give up quickly with you, either.

2. *Satan's power is limited.* In the second temptation, Satan took Jesus to Jerusalem and had Him stand on the pinnacle of the temple. Satan tried to persuade Jesus to jump. Jesus, of course, refused saying that He would not test God. I've often wondered why Satan didn't push Him off the temple after he knew Jesus wouldn't jump. The answer is simple. Satan couldn't do it. His power and authority is limited. God's promise is that He will not allow you to be tempted beyond what you are able to resist. Satan does *not* have carte blanche when it comes to tempting you.

3. *If Satan is resisted, he will flee.* Isn't this wonderful news? "Submit therefore to God. Resist the devil and he will flee from you" (James 4:7). Imagine that. If we

resist Satan he will go away. You can resist him by not
browsing porn sites on the Internet. You can resist him
by not getting an eyeful of magazine covers at your
local convenience store. You can resist him by watching what you allow your eyes to see.

I don't know how long your fight will last. There is
certainly no security in age. I don't believe we'll ever be able
to put ourselves on autopilot and fly past temptation. Joe
Aldrich, former president of Multnomah School of the Bible
wrote, "Have you ever noticed how many men in the Bible
failed in the second half of life? Our enemy is so cunning that
he will wait forty or even fifty years to set a trap."[8]

When I spoke at a men's retreat I divided the guys up
into small groups and told them to go around and say what
tempts them most. We were not going into any detail about
defeats, just temptations. In the group I was observing, there
was a man in his seventies. When it became his turn, a man
in his twenties said to him, "Tell me it goes away." The old
man laughed and said, "I wish I could."

One thing I do know is that your struggle may get
worse before it gets better. Satan will not be pleased with
your renewed commitment to finding freedom. Before you
find the Promised Land of victory, you will encounter a
wilderness experience.

Oswald Chambers said, "It is the process, not the end
that is glorifying to God." For the Israelites leaving Egypt,
it was their wilderness experience where they began to know
God. The Israelites fell again and again, but they were never
in the same spot. They were in-process as they sought the
Promised Land. So it is with you.

And you shall remember all the way which
the Lord your God has led you in the wilderness
these forty years, that He might humble you,
testing you, to know what was in your heart,

whether you would keep His commandments or
not. And He humbled you and let you be hungry,
and fed you with manna which you did not know,
nor did your fathers know, that He might make
you understand that man does not live by bread
alone, but man lives by everything that proceeds
out of the mouth of the Lord (Deut. 8:2–3).

We need to remember that when we face our wilderness experience, we will not be alone. "The steps of a man
are established by the Lord; and He delights in his way.
When he falls, he shall not be hurled headlong; because the
Lord is the One who holds his hand" (Ps. 37:23–24). Notice
the verse does not say "*if* he falls." While your struggle may
get worse, the passage offers wonderful hope. The Lord is
the One who holds your hand!

Remember, however, that Jesus will be with you every
step of the way. It's a road He's traveled before. "And it
came about, when the days were approaching for His ascen-
sion, that He resolutely set His face to go to Jerusalem"
(Luke 9:51). Before Jesus found victory at the cross, He had
to "*resolutely* set His face to go to Jerusalem." Jesus encoun-
tered opposition along the way. You will find opposition on
your journey, too, but you are not alone. Resolutely set your
face towards victory!

FISH AND SECOND CHANCES

Some of you reading this book wonder whether God
could possibly forgive you again. You have failed too many
times in the past. Sexual sin has you in bondage and you have
tried to break free, offering fleeting confessions to God that
never last. Surely you are beyond hope. Before you condemn yourself, you may want to read the records of other
failures recorded in the Bible. I bet the names of Moses,
David, and Peter are familiar to you. Oh yes, and there are
others, too.

Do you remember Jonah? God had given him specific instructions to go to Nineveh and not only did Jonah disobey, he tried to flee to Tarshish which was in the opposite direction. Talk about willful disobedience! It took a few days in the belly of a great fish to help Jonah see things differently, but after he was vomited up onto dry land we read a wonderful verse. "Now the word of the Lord came to Jonah the second time . . ." (Jon. 3:1). Even after Jonah's willful acts of disobedience, God was not through with him. Underline that verse in your Bible because God is not through with you, either. The same God who restored Jonah to ministry wants to restore you, too.

When you have been restored with your sins forgiven, God wants to commission you again. "As obedient children, do not be conformed to the former lusts which were yours in your ignorance, but like the Holy One who called you, be holy yourselves also in all your behavior; because it is written, 'You shall be holy, for I am holy' " (1 Pet. 1:14–15).

Men, we're in the fight of our lives. The casualties caused by pornography and adult entertainment are crippling the Church. It's time for us to claim the victory that Jesus Christ offers. Be holy, because He is holy.

1 Bruce H. Wilkinson, *Victory over Temptation* (Eugene, OR: Harvest House Publishers, 1998), p. 232.

2 "The War Within," *Leadership/92*, Fall Quarter 1992, p. 112.

3 Becky Beane, "The Problem of Pornography," *Jubilee Magazine*, Summer 1998, p. 23.

4 Bill Perkins, *When Good Men Are Tempted* (Grand Rapids, MI: Zondervan Publishing House, 1997), p. 137.

5 Dr. David Jeremiah, "Peter's Restoration" tape, from the series "The Life of Peter," Turning Point radio program.

6 Steve Lawson, *Faith Under Fire* (Wheaton, IL: Crossway Books, 1995), p. 174–177.

7 Charles Stanley, *Winning the War Within* (Nashville, TN: Thomas Nelson Publishers, 1988), p. 123–125.

8 Steve Farrar, *Point Man* (Sisters, OR: Multnomah Press, 1990), p. 66.

15

"But This Is My Daddy"

Train up a child in the way he should go, even when he is old he will not depart from it (Prov. 22:6).

I WAS SITTING AT MY DESK ONE AFTERNOON when an e-mail arrived from a 21-year-old woman named Kristen. She explained how she went to her parent's house and later checked her e-mails from her dad's computer. She discovered an e-mail addressed to her Dad that was pornographic. She deleted it quickly knowing it was a mistake. The next week she got on his computer again and found three more pornographic e-mails. When she looked at his history, she was stunned.

"There were several pornographic sites. One was a site called marriage-match," she wrote. "I checked it out and it promotes affairs for married men and women. I felt physically sick. I am on the net everyday for work, but I never understood how evil it was. I want to help my father before he does something he regrets. Three weeks ago, I had thoughts about finding the right guy, getting married, and having children. Now I don't want to even talk to men. If this can happen to my father, then I see that any man can fall if he strays from his walk . . . but this is my daddy. I am scared. I shouldn't have to deal with this. He shouldn't be doing this. Please, please, please help me."

Kristen's message troubled me greatly. I replied to her message and asked her to call me. When we spoke on the phone later that day she explained that her father was a loving husband who set a godly example in the home. The tears came quickly. When I asked her what her relationship was like with her dad, she said, "I am the biggest daddy's girl there is." She is terrified about the possibility of her mother finding out. And she is scared about confronting her daddy.

How sad that her father, who had set a godly example all of his life, had been caught in sin by his daughter. Everything she believed about godly husbands and fathers was challenged in a single moment. He had been found out.

We have our children for such a short period of time before they leave our homes. It is critical that we set a godly example and run our race with endurance (Heb. 12:1). Too many men today, however, seem to have no interest in running.

As I was going through the westerns at a local video store that carried soft-core pornography from *Playboy* and *Penthouse*, I saw a father walk in with his wife and son. His wife stopped at the posters and began to look through them. The father and son went up one aisle and down another . . . until they came upon the pornographic videos. The father stopped and looked. The son glanced at the videos and instinctively put his hand over his father's eyes.

As I watched this scene unfold, I wondered what kind of values this father would pass on to his son. The father pushed his son's hand away and continued looking at the videos. The son looked up at his father and then turned to look at the videos, too. Together, father and son shared a moment of lust.

"The industry cheapens sex," said Dr. John Spencer, a psychologist who treats sexual offenders. "Kids today are watching so much sex, cybersex or anything else, that they are growing up believing they should attach more importance to it than it is worth."[1] Men, that's what our culture is passing on to the next generation.

Most men see their first pornography as children. Consider the results of my survey of over 100 Christian men. The numbers were startling, but not surprising. Nobody was over 20 years old when they first saw pornography.

Age Exposed	Percentage
Over 30	0%
20–30	0%
15–19	21%
10–14	60%
Under 10	19%

According to the American Family Association, an estimated 70 percent of all pornography ends up in the hands of children. Isn't that staggering? Imagine . . . most boys see hard-core pornography before their very first date. That ought to keep fathers of daughters up at night.

In Dr. Archibald Hart's work *The Sexual Man*, published in 1994, he reported that the average age of a boy's introduction to pornographic material was 15.5 years of age.[2] Lynn Wildmon of the American Family Association said the average age for a child's first exposure is now 11 years old. This number has dropped in recent years because of the Internet. The average age when a man seeks help is 30–35 years old.[3] That's a long time to be held captive.

For some boys, a lifetime of temptation and lust was set in motion because of their father's addiction to pornography. Jack, who is a Sunday school teacher, told me about viewing pornography on the Internet when he felt a presence behind him. He turned around to find his ten-year-old son standing there. How hard it must have been to explain to his son what he was doing. Was it a memory permanently lodged in the memory of his son? The very thought brought Jack to tears.

Tim shared with me that his wife came in the house one day angry because she had caught their ten-year-old son looking at *Hustler* behind their garage. She was furious. Tim told his wife he would have a talk with his son. The talk never happened because Tim didn't know how to confront his son about reading a pornographic magazine that Tim had hidden in the garage.

Two men, two reactions. Tim threw his stash of magazines away while Jack's addiction to pornography on the Internet continued to grow. Even though Jack was filled with guilt and shame at exposing his son to pornography, he would not stop.

We go to great efforts to bring clean water into our homes. Some of us have filtering systems; others pay for water to be delivered. We no longer trust the water that comes from our kitchen sink. Tap water has too many impurities. We want to protect our family and ourselves by keeping the impurities out. Wouldn't it be great if we would do the same with pornography?

Our children need our protection. It's not just the anti-porn advocates that feel this way. "I am very protective of my children," said Glenn Grattiano, an Internet porn site owner. "Just because I'm running _____ Porn Enterprises doesn't mean I'm a sleazebucket. I don't want my children going to this stuff before they are of age."[4] I wonder when Mr. Grattiano thinks his children will be "of age"? I wonder when God thinks they will be "of age"?

Playboy thinks the age is ten. I have proof. A friend of mine has a ten-year-old son who received an invitation in the mail to receive a risk-free issue and two free gifts from *Playboy*. It read, "There's never been a better time to experience the pleasure, passion, and entertaining fun you can only find in *PLAYBOY* — THAN RIGHT NOW." The gifts included "Locker Room Fantasies" and "Playmates Exposed." The invitation even showed the covers of these gifts, which were fairly explicit. Unfortunately for *Playboy*, my friend never let his son see the invitation. Unlike *Playboy*, he cares about the next generation.

Pornography and children are a dangerous combination. Dr. Victor B. Cline, a psychotherapist who specializes in family/marriage counseling and sexual addictions, told about a mother who brought her 13-year-old daughter into his office. It seems her daughter and 14-year-old boyfriend acted out what they saw in pornography found in the home. The consequences included pregnancy, abortion, and depression.[5] That's quite a price to pay for lust.

In another case, two brothers ages nine and ten were secretly watching their parent's stash of pornographic videos while their parents were at work. Later, they forced two younger siblings and a neighborhood boy to watch the videos and strip naked. They forced them to engage in sex acts including oral and anal sex. The abuse lasted for over a year . . . before the parents ever found out.[6]

Dr. Jennings Bryant, part of the 1986 Attorney General's Commission on Pornography, did a study of 600 American males and females in junior high school. Bryant discovered that 91 percent of the males and 82 percent of the females had been exposed to hard-core pornography. He also discovered that 66 percent of the males and 40 percent of the females reported wanting to try out what they had seen.[7]

Of course, the Internet increases exposure of pornography for our children. In 1997, *FamilyPC* magazine surveyed 750 parents about life online. Here's what they discovered:

- 68 percent were concerned that sexually explicit material was being accessed by their children.

- 67 percent had concerns about the marketing to children on the Internet.

- 27 percent allow their children to enter chat rooms and only 68 percent monitored exchanges.[8]

It appears that some parents are asleep at the switch when it comes to the Internet. Donna Rice-Hughes wrote a wonderful book on protecting your children on the Internet called *Kids Online — Protecting Your Children in Cyberspace*.[9] I highly recommend it for parents who have Internet access at home.

Sexual messages are clogging the minds of our children today. They get it from movies, TV, and magazines. The boys learn a distorted view of what they should value in women. It's their beauty and willingness to perform sexual acts that makes women worth dating. Make no mistake about it, pornography sends that message loud and clear.

According to the Kaiser Family Foundation, co-sponsor with Children Now for the "Talking With Kids About Tough Issues" campaign, Dad is not in the top five of the sources where 13–15 year olds learn about sexual issues.[10] If that doesn't floor you, the campaign also reported that 50 percent of the parents have not discussed with their kids about how to know when they are ready for sex. Guys, if you have teenage kids, grab your Bibles and talk to your kids about this critical issue. If you don't, many other influences are too willing to fill in for you.

Young females are saturated today with messages about the importance of beauty from many sources. Have you even seen a teen magazine for girls? The focus is clearly on beauty and sex. That's what makes them of value — who they are on the outside. It wasn't always that way for American girls.

An excerpt from a teenage diary in 1892 read, "Resolved, not to talk about myself or feelings. To think before speaking. To work seriously. To be self-restrained in conversation and actions. Not to let my thoughts wander. To be dignified. Interest myself more in others."

By 1982, things had changed drastically according to one diary, "I will try to make myself better in any way I possibly can with the help of my budget and baby-sitting money. I will lose weight, get new lenses, already got new haircut, good makeup, new clothes and accessories."[11] Does the word "shallow" come to mind?

Not only are girls deceived by advertisements, but also pornography gives them a false picture of the perfect woman. Sadly, few young girls know that a computer has enhanced the pictures. Pornography deceives girls in how they should look and act. Boys want one thing and girls better provide it if they want to keep boys interested. Sex is the name of the game.

Unfortunately, if girls see their father's fascination with pornography, they'll discover that Dad prefers computer-enhanced women over their mother. And the terrible cycle continues.

Men, we have to protect our children from pornography and we have to prepare them for the moment when it crosses their path. It's not a question of "if," it's a question of "when." It may be at a friend's house, it may be in a dumpster, but they'll find pornographic material sometime. Train them what to do when that moment arrives. Train them about making righteous choices.

Child pornography is another horrible evil that feeds on men's lust and plagues our country. The 1954 book *Lolita* hit the screens in 1998. Published in France, the story involves a college professor's obsession with a 12-year-old girl. While it took four years to find an American publisher in the 1950s, it only took two years to find a U.S. distributor of the film in the 1990s.

How could such a movie make it to the big screen? "Pedophilia has become a subject talked about and pushed forward, rightly for the last three years," said Jeremy Irons, who plays the tragically attracted Humbert Humbert. "People want to air this subject, they want to discuss it. And I think the forthcoming production of *Lolita* was a very useful hook to hang the debate on."[12] What? We need to see a movie that is in the middle of an "art" or "pornography" debate to know that we should stay as far away from pedophilia as possible? Amazingly, one critic of the movie said it wasn't sexy enough! Sex between a college professor and a 12 year old is not sexy enough?

"I object because according to press reports, the film's director, Adrian Lyne, set out to make *Lolita* as sexually explicit as he could, without violating the law and losing the 'R-rating' his contract required," said Robert Peters, president of Morality in Media. "I also object because Lyne's remake of *Lolita* portrays having sex with a minor to be the most sexually exciting experience an adult heterosexual male — and a female child — could imagine."[13]

Are we out of control? Is it possible that pedophilia is becoming mainstream? At Cornell University, a course is offered called, "The Sexual Child." According to the campus newspaper, the syllabus "reads like a veritable who's-who of pro-pedophilia academics and activists." Materials for the course include the pro-pedophilia book *Child Loving*. Bizarre? It gets worse.

Course instructor Ellis Hanson said, "The erotic fascination with children is ubiquitous. One could hardly read a newspaper or turn on a television without feeling obliged to accept, study, and celebrate it."[14] The only thing I feel obliged to do is to make sure he stays away from children.

Bookstores across the country carry books with pictures of nude children taken by various photographers. I read the on-line review of one such book written by a man who had purchased the work. "This book is a definite turn-on," he wrote. "I have fallen in love with nearly every pubescent and pre-pubescent girl [the author] depicts. It is incredibly sexually arousing, leaving me with no choice but to dream, by myself and in private, of the wonderful privilege it would be to have the freedom to love these young ladies fully, sexually, and in real life without concern for society's taboos and chastisement." He also wrote that ladies over the age of 16 "no longer seem attractive." Certainly these are words from the pen of a pedophile. Men, if you haven't made the discovery yet, the next generation is in trouble.

Children are an incredible blessing from God, and as fathers we need to prepare them for righteous living. In this country, it is harder today than at any other time in the history of this nation. The task is great and needs the commitment of Dad. Do your job well — the next generation is counting on you.

1 "On the Dark Side: The Hidden Costs," *Fort Lauderdale Sun-Sentinel*, November 14, 1997.

2 Dr. Archibald D. Hart, *The Sexual Man* (Dallas, TX: Word Publishing, 1994), p. 40.

3 Lynn Wildmon, "Spouses" cassette tape, Sexual Wholeness Conference, Memphis, Tennessee, 1998.

4 "Sex Site Owners Urge Caution," *USA Today*, August 19, 1997.

5 Dr. David Jeremiah, "Peter's Restoration" tape, from the series "The Life of Peter," Turning Point radio program.

6 Ibid.

7 Ibid., p. 11.

8 Donna Rice-Hughes, *Kids Online — Protecting Your Children in Cyberspace* (Grand Rapids, MI: Revell, 1998), p. 131.

9 Rice-Hughes, *Kids Online — Protecting Your Children in Cyberspace* (Grand Rapids, MI: Revell, 1998).

10 "Families Discussing Sexual Issues, Survey Says," *Dallas Morning News*, March 1, 1999.

11 "Teen Girls No Longer Enjoy an Age of Innocence," *USA Today*, October 6, 1997, p. 4D.

12 Robert Bianco, "New Lolita Reignites an Old Debate," *USA Today*, July 14, 1998.

13 Press release, "Morality in Media Denounces Adrian Lyne's Remake of *Lolita*," July 30, 1998.

14 "Pedophilia 101 at Cornell," *Cornell University Campus Report*, October 1998.

16

The Wounded Wife

An excellent wife, who can find? For her
worth is far above jewels (Prov. 31:10).

GUYS, THIS BOOK WOULD NOT BE COMPLETE without the words
of a wife. I want you to hear firsthand the destruction we
cause to the women we love the most — our wives — when
we continue to lose the battle to sexual temptation.

"Emily" is not her real name. She is, however, a real
person whose anonymity I have sworn to protect. I met her
over the phone and we talked several times after that. In her
words I heard an incredible love for Jesus. I also heard her
pain, inflicted by her husband who is trapped in the deception of pornography. The woman is real, her story is real and
her pain is real. And if you are losing the battle to pornography and adult entertainment, your wife may one day write
the same words. May it never be.

EMILY'S STORY

I write this out of love. Love for the porn addict, love
for his wife, and most of all for the children. I pray this
chapter is used for God's glory and honor, that it might

somehow prevent families from being destroyed.

I remember listening to a panel of women James Dobson had on his radio program. They talked about being married for over 20 years and discovering their husbands were involved in pornography. It seemed so unfathomable to me that someone could be deceived for so long. I remember thinking how stupid those women were. Little did I realize I would be one of those women less than a month later.

It was like a birth process. Pain, agony, sweat, tears, hours of intense hurt, and finally truth. My husband is a porn addict. I heard it. I reacted. For two weeks I was numb. Numb to after 20+ years knowing something was wrong, but not knowing what. A relief to finally know the truth. A relief to now live in reality — in light and truth rather than the unreality of darkness and deception. My husband would never tell me the secrets of his past before our marriage. I always thought if I loved him enough some day he would tell me. If I loved him enough. . . .

We always had a difficult marriage. My husband was always withdrawn and quiet. I thought I could help him. I was outgoing, attractive, and spontaneous. In our marriage I could never do anything good enough. I was constantly criticized and put down. I thought it was me so I started a self-improvement program, more counseling, more seminars. I learned more was never enough. My world stopped, knowing something had died in me.

My husband always seemed to be "tuned out" — in another world. He worked long hours and often fell into bed at 2 a.m. I missed him. I begged him to come home. I raised the kids as he pursued his career. I told myself I needed to help him. I poured my heart and soul into his endeavor — supporting and encouraging. There were still problems. When he was home he would go into his office and read his books, newspapers, and reports, and again I would cry myself to sleep. I had others confront him. I gave this man every chance to tell me about his pornography addiction. Lies weave other lies. Secrets kill. Comparisons kill. I feel

every time he looked at an image and masturbated he took
away a part of me that God intended to be mine. I remember
seeing him masturbate and he was in his own world, set on
his own pleasure, stimulated and excited by images of
women he didn't know. It was a feeling of betrayal and
heart-wrenching emptiness that a woman feels when she
learns that her husband is living a lie.

Pornography tears at the very thread of a woman and her
femininity. My heart was ripped and uprooted — thrown
somewhere into a desert with no place to find refuge. It's as if
I wasn't enough. Not sexy enough. Not beautiful enough. Not
thin enough. Not exciting enough. Women get significance
from their relationships with their husbands and when he turns
to another for satisfaction it cuts her deeply at the core.

I started buying sexy nighties, acting sexier, and suddenly I realized I was bowing down to an idol. It hurt that he
chose not to tell me . . . to not allow me to come alongside
him as his helper. To this day he refuses to see the pain that
he caused. It amazes me as a wife how we are involved in
every other area of a man's life — his profit margin, his
ability to manage, everything — but when it comes to
pornography, it's hidden in deception. A man's way seems
right to a man. Porn addiction is very selfish. It takes and
takes and doesn't give back. It's all for the user's pleasure.

Another lie is that porn does not hurt anyone. Such a
web of deception. "And they, having become callous, have
given themselves over to sensuality, for the practice of every
kind of impurity with greediness" (Eph. 4:19). There are
consequences and the stakes get higher. It takes one lie to
cover another. It saddens me how men can compartmental-
ize this sin. He has the little wife over here with precious
children and this nasty sin over here for his private time,
justifying it because he still loves his wife and children. You
can't walk simultaneously in the darkness and the light.

I'm a wife. I'm a wife of a porn addict. I'm relieved to
know what it is, though I always knew something was
wrong. Tears. Pain. Disgust. Betrayal. To face the death of

a husband would be better than this. A widow has the support of the church. A porn addict leaves shame and divorce. It would be easier if he were dead. We wouldn't have to face the public humiliation and shame.

Today is a new day. It's early morning and I must get breakfast for my children. I take each day as it comes now. Just for today. My husband still chooses his sin and refuses to take responsibility for it. I have to let him go and let the Lord deal with him. I can no longer be his excuse, his enabler. It's a new day and I'm moving on and my Deliverer is by my side. He is faithful. He will never leave me nor forsake me. He will never break His promise. To a woman who has been betrayed, this is my comfort. Hear my cry.

"EMILY"

"Emily" and I spoke briefly when I met her to pick up the rough draft of the chapter. After 20+ years of marriage and children, Emily is still physically attractive — what some men would call a "trophy wife," though I've always hated that term. More so than her physical beauty is a heart committed to God. I could see so clearly that her worth is far above jewels, as Proverbs 31:10 describes an excellent wife. Sadly for "Emily" the comparison stops there. In verse 11 we read that "the heart of her husband trusts in her, and he will have no lack of gain." Instead "Emily's" husband knows loss because he was not willing to trust her. Not willing to take down the walls of deception and be transparent to his wife, the helper God gave him.

It hurt me to go through her notes, wanting instead to gently place them back into the envelope. It was if I had stolen her diary and was invading the most private and painful part of her life. Yet "Emily's" heart is to walk in the light — to be used by God so that other women will not one day share the same hurt. Is it a story your wife could write? Is this just the story of "Emily," or will the woman you stood next to before God in marriage one day cry the same tears. Indeed . . . may it never be.

Epilogue

Loose Ends

Therefore do not let sin reign in your mortal
body that you should obey its lusts (Rom. 6:12).

WRITING THIS BOOK WAS VERY DIFFICULT. Most men think
about sex during the day, but for me it was even harder. I read
anything I could get dealing with pornography. I got a few
resources from Amazon.com, the on-line book distributor.
One of the features of the service is to recommend titles that
you should be interested in based on previous purchases.
You ought to see what they recommend for me. It's pretty
disgusting. If it weren't for this book, I would have a lot of
explaining to do if anyone saw the list of recommendations.

I spent time on the Internet searching for material. I
interviewed over 50 women who had been in the industry.
Some of them told me some pretty graphic stuff. While I
always tried to find resources that would not be titillating, I
sometimes failed.

When books I had ordered arrived in the mail, I told my
wife to hide them in my office so the kids could not see them.
One contained useful information with pornographic pictures.

I made sure my wife was with me as I went through the book.

When I got what I needed out of that book, I destroyed it. Sure, I didn't want it to fall into my son's hands, but guys, I didn't want it to fall into my hands anymore. I had no reason to look at it. I got what I needed. If I went back, it would be for reasons of lust. I didn't want the temptation. It was time to flee.

I also spent time in chat rooms and porn sites to see how they operated. Though valuable from a research perspective, I saw things that took my mind places where it should not have gone. I mentioned earlier that things we have been exposed to tempt us most. I know that from firsthand experience. I was never tempted by porn on the Internet until I went into my very first porn site. To protect myself, I now have an Internet service provider at home that blocks offensive sites. I want to make good decisions. I want to live a life pleasing to the Lord. I want to be an ambassador for Christ to those who know me. I can't do that if porn on the Internet is choking me.

Do I know for certain if I had unblocked Internet access in my home, I would lose the battle? No, I don't know that. If I followed the steps outlined in this book, I would be victorious. For me, however, I would rather not face an unnecessary temptation. Remember that Romans 13:14 tells us not to make a provision for the flesh in regard to its lusts. Guys, unblocked Internet access *is* making a provision for the flesh! Some of you need Internet access at home. If you do, protect yourself.

The time I spent talking to women who came out of the sex industry was helpful but their stories broke my heart. One woman who is still dancing, Billie Jo, goes by the stage name "Country." Billie Jo and I talked for over two hours. I listened as she told me about her family and her life. She never mentioned a father or a husband.

I think she enjoyed talking to me because I never came on to her. I just asked her questions and made good eye contact as she spoke. Billie Jo confided that she wasn't used to that kind of treatment from men. I asked her if she had any dreams. She looked at me, took another puff of her cigarette, and said, "Yea — heaven. I want to dance in heaven because my heaven on earth has not been so good." She was 50 years old and still trying to make money by fulfilling the lusts of men. Billie Jo desperately wanted heaven but didn't have a clue about God. I made sure she found out about God and where to get help, but I have not seen her since so I don't know what decisions she made about her life and future.

Everything I've written brings me back to the women. They are tragic victims in this ugly mess. They are not bimbos or criminals. They are victims kept in bondage by men who know all about bondage. I told my wife, Kathy, that I wished every man could spend time talking to these women and hear the truth about their lives. I'm convinced that the truth would drive Christian men to their knees, pleading for forgiveness. That's the impact that it had on me.

Men, the battle will be more intense in the future. As I said before, we are surrounded. It's too easy to find pornography today. We have to protect ourselves. I believe righteous living in America has never been more difficult. While our culture allows moral changes, the word of God does not. In Isaiah 40:8 it is written, "The grass withers, the flower fade, but the word of our God stands forever." His word is true today.

Commit *now* to godly living. You may have some loose ends in your past that need to be dealt with. Are you being held captive in the grip of pornography? This is the time to deal with it. Are you fearful for your future because porn has been a part of your past? It's time to deal with it. Are you concerned about the legacy that you'll pass to the next generation? It's time to deal with it.

A.W. Tozer wrote, "The reason why many are still troubled, still seeking, still making little forward progress is because they have not yet come to the end of themselves."[1]

Some men come to the end of themselves when their family is destroyed. Fortunately, you don't need to wait that long.

God alone can set you free. The journey begins when He sees the heart of a repentant sinner. Confess your sin and your struggle to God. Ask daily for His protection. Ask daily for His strength. Each new day put on the full armor of God. Discover the victorious life that is found in Christ.

Along the way you will stumble. As I mentioned in the introduction, your addiction wasn't created in a day. You still have a tough fight ahead. In moments of failure, confess the setbacks to God and move forward.

Men are sometimes hesitant to confess sin to God that they have brought before Him previously. They wonder how God could possibly forgive them — again. I love what Jack Hayford once said on his radio program.

"Suppose I had committed a particular sin 292 times in the past, and then do it again," said Hayford. "How can God think I am sincere when I have sinned again and again and then repented and asked for forgiveness again and again, and yet I have done the same thing another time? I am ashamed and don't even feel right in approaching Him. I delay for awhile, but finally I face up to my sin and say to God in sorrow, 'I did it again.' Do you know what God would respond? He would ask, 'You did what again?' "[2]

What a picture of God's grace and forgiveness! In Psalm 103:12 it is written, "As far as the east is from the west, so far has He removed our transgressions from us." Don't allow problems to derail your progress. God wants you to be victorious!

As I was bringing this book to a close, my wife asked what I was planning on writing next. It's funny, but I have no grand desire to be an author. Nor do I feel God's leading to be an author. This book, however, I had to write. I had to write it for you — and I had to write it for me.

Pornography and adult entertainment once had me in its grip. In writing this book, I've reviewed the lowest moments of my life. They were moments that carried incredible shame. Moments which brought me to tears as I wrote. Yet throughout this project, I held tightly to one indisputable truth — I am forgiven.

The same can be true for you. How, you wonder? *Adult Video News* attorney Clyde DeWitt said, "The sharpest arrow in an adult-retailer's quiver, of course, is the First Amendment."[3] Imagine that. The strongest weapon the sex industry has is the First Amendment. Our strongest weapon is the Sword of the Spirit, which is the word of God. It may seem like we are outnumbered, but the weapons we wage war with come from God. God's word tells us that we can be forgiven. All we have to do is ask.

"For the Lord hears the needy, and does not despise His who are prisoners" (Ps. 69:33). You can be deceived into believing that God could not possibly forgive you . . . again. Yet the Lord does indeed hear the needy and He will not despise men who are prisoners to pornography. The wounds in His hands and feet are eternal reminders of His love for you.

It is my prayer that you will find freedom in Jesus Christ, the One who paid your debt in full. You've embraced the sin, now embrace the Savior.

1 Bruce H. Wilkinson, editor, *Victory Over Temptation* (Eugene, OR: Harvest House Publishers, 1998), p. 12.
2 Frank R. Beaudine, *Ultimate Success* (Wheaton, IL: Tyndale House Publishers, 1997), p. 81.
3 "There Are Courts and There Are Courts," *Adult Video News*, May 1998.

Endorsements

As any military man knows, when one goes into war there is a need to be trained and ready for the encounter. The book *The Silent War* is a much-needed writing for both Christians and non-Christians because of the addiction of pornography and lust that pervades our world today. If you want to be ready to win the battle and the war, *The Silent War* is a must read.

> Brigadier General Dick Abel, USAF (Ret.)
> Executive Director, Military Ministry
> A Ministry of Campus Crusade for
> Christ International

The Silent War is a look behind enemy lines at the largest battle men and their families face today, that very few have the courage to talk about: sexual temptation. Henry Rogers captures the wake of destruction that pornography leaves behind — broken marriages, calloused men, emotionally exhausted women, and disheartened children. Yet, Henry also gives hope and inspiration to the weary traveler trapped in this web of lies and deceit. There is forgiveness and freedom found in a personal relationship with God through Jesus Christ. *The Silent War* has it all. Every man and woman concerned about the decay of decency in our culture must read *The Silent War*.

> Daniel E. Panetti, Esq., Executive Director
> Dallas Association for Decency

Many Christian men desire holiness in their thoughts and actions but feel defeated and alone when it comes to facing pornography. Henry Rogers has written a strong, biblically sound book. His style is refreshingly honest and direct, sharing both personal experience and extensive biblical and psychological research. It offers hope and victory. I recommend this book not only for men seeking a way out but also to parents who need to prepare their sons from a young age to navigate the rough waters of modern society.

> Luis Palau, President
> Luis Palau Ministries

The Silent War tackles the tough issue of pornography and its impact on Christian men. Too many men are losing the fight when God wants us all to be victorious. Henry Rogers understands the problem and clearly communicates the solution. Get the book to help other men or get it to help yourself.

> Joe Gibbs, Owner, Joe Gibbs Racing
> Former coach, Washington Redskins
> NFL Hall of Fame Coach